Cambridge Elements ≡

Elements in Experimental Political Science
edited by
James N. Druckman
Northwestern University

QUALITY CONTROL

Experiments on the Microfoundations of Retrospective Voting

Austin Hart
American University
J. Scott Matthews
Memorial University of Newfoundland

Shaftesbury Road, Cambridge CB2 8EA, United Kingdom

One Liberty Plaza, 20th Floor, New York, NY 10006, USA

477 Williamstown Road, Port Melbourne, VIC 3207, Australia

314–321, 3rd Floor, Plot 3, Splendor Forum, Jasola District Centre, New Delhi – 110025, India

103 Penang Road, #05–06/07, Visioncrest Commercial, Singapore 238467

Cambridge University Press is part of Cambridge University Press & Assessment, a department of the University of Cambridge.

We share the University's mission to contribute to society through the pursuit of education, learning and research at the highest international levels of excellence.

www.cambridge.org
Information on this title: www.cambridge.org/9781009357036

DOI: 10.1017/9781009357005

First published 2023

A catalogue record for this publication is available from the British Library.

ISBN 978-1-009-35703-6 Paperback
ISSN 2633-3368 (online)
ISSN 2633-335X (print)

Quality Control

Experiments on the Microfoundations of Retrospective Voting

Elements in Experimental Political Science

DOI: 10.1017/9781009357005
First published online: May 2023

Austin Hart
American University

J. Scott Matthews
Memorial University of Newfoundland

Author for correspondence: Austin Hart, ahart@american.edu

Abstract: Conventional models of voting behavior depict individuals who judge governments for how the world unfolds during their time in office. This phenomenon of retrospective voting requires that individuals integrate and appraise streams of performance information over time. Yet past experimental studies short-circuit this "integration-appraisal" process. In this Element, we develop a new framework for studying retrospective voting and present eleven experiments building on that framework. Notably, when we allow integration and appraisal to unfold freely, we find little support for models of "blind retrospection." Although we observe clear recency bias, we find respondents who are quick to appraise and who make reasonable use of information cues. Critically, they regularly employ benchmarking strategies to manage complex, variable, and even confounded streams of performance information. The results highlight the importance of centering the integration-appraisal challenge in both theoretical models and experimental designs and begin to uncover the cognitive foundations of retrospective voting.

This Element also has an additional material availabe @
https://www.cambridge.org/HartMatthewsSupplementaryMaterials

Keywords: retrospective voting, voting behavior, experimental design, democratic accountability, external validity

Isbns: 9781009357036 (PB), 9781009357005 (OC)
Issns: 2633-3368 (online), 2633-335X (print)

Contents

1 Introduction

Among the most widespread regularities in the study of political behavior is the relationship between the state of the world and the vote. When times are good, incumbents tend to win reelection; when times are bad, sitting governments tend to pay the price at the polls. This phenomenon of retrospective voting – citizens registering their appraisals of past performance in their judgment of incumbents – motivates a vast empirical literature.[1] Past research finds voters around the world taking governments to task for outcomes in areas as diverse as economic growth, the prosecution of wars, and the making of prudent preparations for natural disasters. Yet it remains unclear if voters' judgments sensibly differentiate competent from incompetent incumbents. Notably, Achen and Bartels (2016) argue that voters' assessments reflect their idiosyncratic moods about the state of the world and that events beyond the incumbent's control – e.g., droughts or global financial crises – weigh heavily on these moods. Retrospective voting, in this view, is more akin to kicking the dog over a missed promotion than a mechanism for political accountability.

Debate about the normative significance of retrospective voting follows from uncertainty about how – and how well – voters manage what we term the "integration-appraisal" task. Retrospective voters of any stripe must reduce streams of performance information into a summary evaluation of incumbent competence. This necessitates the *integration* of information streams into a cognitively manageable impression of the state of things during an incumbent's term and the formation of an *appraisal* based on that impression. Theories of retrospective voting describe the process by which voters might – reliably or otherwise – manage integration and appraisal, but existing frameworks for studying retrospective voting are ill-equipped to test these arguments.

Numerous observational studies consider voters' capacity to meet various information-processing challenges inherent to retrospective voting (e.g., Quinn and Woolley, 2001; Ebeid and Rodden, 2006; Kayser and Peress, 2012; Stiers et al., 2020). However, because nature does not generally assign performance outcomes randomly, and because observational researchers typically cannot disentangle an incumbent's contribution to those outcomes from exogenous spillover, concerns about causal identification abound. This, of course, is the opening line of the experimentalist's sales pitch. A more tangible virtue of experimentation in the study of retrospective voting is the method's relative capacity to shed light on the integration-appraisal process. The ability to

---

[1] Retrospective voting is sometimes called "performance voting," and terms like "economic voting" refer to retrospective voting in a particular domain. See Healy and Malhotra (2013) for a review of the literature on retrospective voting.

manipulate the valence, variance, and source of performance outcomes – and the context within which those outcomes are observed – allows the experimentalist to study the psychology of retrospection in settings that are often difficult to observe in the "real world." In our view, experimental control of this nature is critical to advancing the study of retrospective voting.

Surprisingly, experimental research into the microfoundations of retrospection is quite limited. Those experiments that do exist generally simplify away one or both phases of integration and appraisal. In a typical design, researchers might expose participants to a static, "pre-integrated" summary of performance (e.g., GDP growth) and a "pre-appraised" interpretation thereof (e.g., "the rate of growth is good"). Thus, in both the typical observational and experimental studies, we may see that individuals respond to performance cues in judging an incumbent, but the core evaluative process remains largely unobserved.

In this Element, we explore the microfoundations of retrospective voting. We develop an abstract experimental framework that captures the streaming quality of information confronted by voters and *requires* them to arrive at their own appraisal of the information they encounter (Section 3). We present results from eleven experiments addressing foundational questions about the mechanisms driving the retrospective vote. We consider voters' basic capacities in assessing a variable stream of performance information (Section 4); how retrospective voters confront the challenge of interdependence, where spillover from extra-local forces obscures an incumbent's efforts (Section 5); and how voters seek out and use heuristics, that is, simplifying information about performance, in the integration-appraisal process (Section 6). Given our reliance on an abstract experimental design we also advance a case for abstract experimental approaches in the study of retrospective voting. In Section 2, we outline the logic that justifies such designs and explain how their unrealism facilitates, rather than impedes, the making of new generalizations.

1.1 Retrospective Voting As Integration and Appraisal

The literature contains scores of models of retrospective voting, some more explicit than others (e.g., Downs, 1957; Key, 1966; Fiorina, 1981; Ferejohn, 1986). For Berry and Howell (2007), retrospective voting is simply "the proposition that citizens examine whether the state of the world has improved under a politician's watch and vote accordingly" (p. 844). In their landmark study of economic voting, Duch and Stevenson (2008) proceed formally, presenting a model that rests on a specific decomposition of the variance of economic growth. The unifying thread, and the foundation of our account, is the idea that voters' evaluations of the state of the world motivate their decision to reelect or replace an elected official. This implies that voters acquire information about prevailing conditions and use at least some of it to form judgments of their government's performance. As those judgments improve, so too does the likelihood that the voter supports reelection.

This process unfolds in an environment where voters encounter streams of performance cues – e.g., quarterly jobs reports or news stories about crime – across the timeline of electoral politics. Whether these flows are sporadic, uneven, or confounded by external spillover, acknowledging the streaming quality of this information highlights the necessity for retrospective voters to undertake some sequence of integration and appraisal. Before judging an incumbent, retrospective voters must *integrate* some of the information they encounter into a summary impression. Consciously or otherwise, this requires weighing information of varying relevance and quality. Voters must also render an *appraisal* of their impressions and ultimately apply that to the vote decision (cf. Downs, 1957, pp. 45–46). Consider a voter concerned with the price of groceries in their state. Over time, they are exposed – via direct experience and mediated reports – to information they may recognize as bearing on food prices. How do they weigh and combine these diverse indicators to form an overall summary of affordability during their governor's administration? How do they decide whether that summary indicates good or bad performance?

Our approach to retrospective voting through the framework of integration and appraisal is significant for several reasons. First, because the task is fundamental to retrospective voting, the integration-appraisal framework encompasses a wide range of more specific behavioral-psychological and informational assumptions. The task obtains whether voters' appraisals of performance are myopic (e.g., Healy and Lenz, 2014) or based on integration over longer time horizons (e.g., Stiers et al., 2020). It allows that voters may be relatively discerning (e.g., Hellwig, 2001) or indiscriminate (e.g., Achen and Bartels, 2016) in identifying their incumbent's contributions to performance outcomes. The integration-appraisal framework encompasses both the assumption that voters seek to *sanction* their governors for past outcomes – to incentivize good performance (Key, 1966) – and the possibility that voters use past outcomes to infer incumbent competence, thus informing the *selection* of quality rulers (Duch and Stevenson, 2008). And the task holds whether voters encounter performance information directly or that information is mediated by friends, television, or Twitter. Performance necessarily unfolds over time, even if its level is static. Whether relying on direct experience or the reports of others, and whether information arrives as "raw data" (e.g., unemployment is 9 percent) or suggests an evaluative interpretation (e.g., "Have you heard how high unemployment is?"), integration across multiple pieces of performance information is required.

Second, unpacking the integration-appraisal task clarifies the problematic nature of appraising performance, even when doing so involves only one piece of information. A Canadian voter suffering respiratory symptoms must wait a week to see their family doctor. Is the public health care system performing well or poorly? Answering such questions requires an account of how voters judge the quality of a given level of observed performance.

Third, the framework highlights the difficulty of forming a summary impression from multiple pieces of information. The need for voters to integrate across streams of variable performance increases the potential burden of retrospective voting relative to a world – like the one found in many experimental tests of retrospective voting – that simply reveals pure signals of incumbent competence. Some strategy must be applied, consciously or otherwise, to weigh and reduce the multiplicity of performance cues into a manageable impression. This challenge is aggravated in an era of globalization, where performance *here* is increasingly tied to actors and actions *over there*. This problem of interdependence, or spillover, makes it more difficult for voters to identify their incumbent's efforts. To be sure, the "rule" voters apply in confronting this challenge may be normatively sound (e.g., systematic weighing of discrete performances) or quite arbitrary (e.g., attending only to whatever information is cognitively available when making a judgment). Our argument is simply that the availability of multiple cues, and the confounding of those cues by spillover from multiple actors, is a generic feature of retrospective voting.

In conceptualizing performance evaluation in terms of the integration-appraisal task, we emphasize that we are not advancing a novel theory of retrospective voting. On the contrary, we regard the assumption that voters observe, combine, and evaluate indicators of performance as an essential feature of *all* retrospective voting theories, including those that assume voters manage the task poorly. With the experiments reported in this Element, we evaluate a family of specific theories that, despite their varying assumptions, share a general premise: that retention of incumbents is related to their performance *via* a process of integration and appraisal of performance cues.

In summary, retrospective voting theory implies that voters encounter information bearing on the state of the world that they use to judge government performance.[2] An important feature of that information is that it generally manifests as a stream of cues. The retrospective voter somehow utilizes the information in the stream to arrive at an impression of performance and forms

---

[2] Discussing the integration-appraisal task as a linear, two-step sequence is only an expository convenience. Alternatively, voters may first appraise incoming bits of information and then integrate over appraisals before rendering a final appraisal (see Section 4.3.2).

an appraisal that they apply come Election Day. The key point is that both integration and appraisal are inherent to this process.

1.2 Prior Experiments in Retrospective Voting

In view of the vastness of the retrospective voting literature, experimental tests are surprisingly uncommon and recent. A systematic search of the political science literature uncovers just thirty-four published articles containing experimental tests of retrospective voting.[3] All but four of these were published after 2010, and roughly a third do not involve questions that require the manipulation of performance evaluations in any way.[4]

Studies that do explicitly "treat" performance evaluations generally short-circuit the integration-appraisal task in whole or in part, with subjects encountering information that requires no integration and/or no appraisal. Treatments often combine high-level verbal summaries of performance outcomes in a real or hypothetical setting with an explicit or implicit appraisal. For example, in Tilley and Hobolt's (2011) study of attributions of responsibility in retrospective voting, participants in one condition read: "Experts say that not only have economic conditions deteriorated a lot over the last year, but the British economy is doing considerably worse than most other countries" (p. 323). The statement provides an integrated summary of economic performance; it also conveys an implicit appraisal through its evaluative tone ("conditions deteriorated a lot") and the unfavorable comparisons to other economies (see also Sigelman et al., 1991; Klasnja and Tucker, 2013; Malhotra and Margalit, 2014; Simonovitz, 2015).

Several experiments provide similar pre-integrated summaries of performance outcomes but without cues to guide participants' appraisal. Clinton and Grissom (2015), for example, examine the impact of revealed performance on evaluation of educational institutions in Tennessee. Their treatments inform participants about the percentages of students "performing at grade level or better on Tennessee's end-of-grade math tests" (p. 365). This allows participants to form their own appraisals of competence even as it obviates the need for voters to reduce streams of performance cues into a summary of their own.

Finally, some experiments treat performance evaluations with information that is not summarized but nonetheless provide a weak basis for conclusions

---

[3] Using the Web of Science database, in February 2022 we queried political science journal abstracts for intersections of "experiment" with "retrospective voting," "economic voting," or any of the various related word combinations (e.g., "economic evaluation"). We augmented the results with pieces of which we were already aware. We reviewed the ~150 abstracts to determine which involved experimental work on retrospective voting.

[4] Some seek instead to manipulate the *salience* of performance evaluations to examine the existence of retrospective voting rather than its microfoundations per se.

regarding citizens' handling of the integration-appraisal task. For example, Bhandari et al.'s (2023) field experimental study of the impact of benchmarks on retrospective voting treats participants with information regarding legislator performance along five separate dimensions. Yet tests of the impact of the performance information rely on comparisons with a control condition in which no performance information was presented. As such, it is unclear whether the treatment effect reflects the acquisition – and integration – of new performance information or simply the priming of performance considerations.

None of this is meant to suggest that these studies fail to address the research questions on which they focus. On the contrary, these studies offer key insights in the retrospective voting literature. Our point is that those insights rely on designs that cannot speak directly to voters' capacity to integrate across multiple pieces of performance information and to form appraisals that are unaided by explicit or implicit cues. In this sense, the far-reaching literature on retrospective voting rests on assumptions about an integration-appraisal task that has rarely been studied in a controlled setting.

An important exception is Huber et al.'s (2012) study of bias in retrospective evaluation. The logic of the design is to study performance evaluation in a highly simplified and abstract setting that "allows [them] to understand whether suboptimal decision making is a function of the complexity of the real world . . . or is instead due to basic limitations in individuals' retrospective abilities" (p. 721). Participants in these studies play an incentivized game that centers on the decision to replace or retain an "allocator." The allocator provides tokens as payments that subjects later redeem for cash. The allocator's underlying competence, or type, is drawn randomly from a known distribution; the payment in each period is drawn from a distribution centered on the allocator's type. Participants observe a sequence of sixteen payments before electing to retain their allocator for another sixteen payments or draw another at random from a known distribution.

From our perspective, the key feature of Huber and colleagues' design is that performance information is conveyed as a stream of discrete outcomes, unaccompanied by an explicit or implicit appraisal.[5] Participants must, therefore, form an impression on their own. Having formed such an impression, the task of judging whether the allocator clears the bar for retention is also left to participants. In a way that is seemingly unique in the literature, the incentivized

---

[5] As we discuss in Section 3, the game's instructions allow participants to infer an "optimal decision rule for risk-neutral participants" (Huber et al., 2012, p. 723), which then implies an appraisal of average performance. In our view, this feature of the design leaves considerable room for participants to arrive at independent appraisals of performance, though we expect appraisals to be informed by the instructions (see the discussion in Section 4.1.1).

allocator design leaves the central information-processing task of retrospective voting entirely to the participant.[6]

1.3 Our Experimental Approach

The experimental studies in this Element build on – and go considerably beyond – Huber and colleagues' basic framework to address new questions and long-standing debates about retrospective voting (notably, doing so leads us to draw quite different conclusions; see, especially, Section 7.1). Here, we outline our approach and describe our experiments in general terms, leaving the details to later sections. For reference, Table 1 summarizes the eleven experiments we present in this Element.

Table 1 Summary of retrospective voting experiments

Experiment	Performance streams (n)	Motivating questions
1	Single (248)	Given a stream of variable performance output, can participants discriminate between competent and incompetent incumbents?
2	Single (403)	Does performance variability inhibit retrospective voting?
3	Single (719)	Negativity bias: Are participants more inclined to punish poor performance than to reward good performance?
4	Single (764)	Recency bias: Do participants place more weight on performance late in an incumbent's term?
5	Multiple (849)	How do participants judge an incumbent whose performance is confounded by a high- versus low-variance disturbance?
6	Multiple (368)	Can participants assess an unobstructed performance signal without reference to an exogenous disturbance?

---

[6] Huber et al. (2012) are largely silent on the theoretical significance of their unique design in this regard, though they recognize their design requires participants to "infer" performance from observed "payouts" (p. 720).

Table 1 (cont.)

Experiment	Performance streams (n)	Motivating questions
7	Multiple (550)	How do participants judge an incumbent whose performance is obscured by a complex disturbance?
8	Multiple (720)	Given a choice among summary measures of performance, do participants actively seek "pre-benchmarked" indicators?
9	Multiple (1,376)	Does exposure to summary reports of incumbent competence mitigate the benchmarking response?
10	Single (394)	Given a choice among benchmarks of varying quality, do participants select good benchmarks?
11	Multiple (918)	Do participants adjust their comparisons for "shocked" benchmarks?

Our framework asks participants to serve as factory managers observing the performance of a new worker (or workers). After sixteen weeks of production, the participant must elect to extend their "incumbent" worker's contract or to hire a replacement. The incumbent's competence is unknown at the outset, the stream of production is variable, and information regarding incumbent performance is sometimes confounded or obscured by the presence of coworkers; the game ends with a choice of consequence between the incumbent and a lesser-known replacement. We attempt to motivate participants to maximize worker performance by assigning cash bonuses in proportion to the number of units their workers produce. We do not suggest an appraisal of worker performance, except when doing so is necessary to answer a question of interest (i.e., in Exps. 3 and 11).

The principal virtue of the factory-worker metaphor, relative to Huber et al.'s (2012) allocator, is that we can draw on stereotyped knowledge of workers and factories to simplify exposition of the features of our experimental environments. This gives us the flexibility to address a wide range of fundamental questions in the retrospective voting literature with only minor changes to game design and task instructions. The experiments in Section 4 (Exps. 1–4), for example, all consider an individual's capacity to integrate and appraise over a single stream of incumbent performance information. With slight adjustments to the presentation of information or the parameters of worker performance, we can test a range of hypotheses, concerning, for example, recency bias (Healy and Lenz, 2014; Stiers et al., 2020) and negativity bias (Baumeister et al., 2001).

The flexibility of our experimental framework – and the familiarity of the factory analogy – also enables us to create more complex tasks without short-circuiting the integration-appraisal process. This is critical as we explore the challenge of retrospection under interdependence. How individuals evaluate government performance when external spillover – the coming together of endogenous and exogenous streams of performance – obscures the incumbent's efforts is a central focus in recent observational research on retrospective voting. Yet we know of no experiment that asks participants to integrate and appraise over multiple and/or confounded streams of information. Section 5's experiments (Exps. 5–8) introduce the performance of peer or "comparator" workers, some of whom arrive late or depart early, to obscure the incumbent's efforts. In so doing, these experiments permit diagnostic tests of three conventional models of retrospective voting under interdependence: rational discounting (Duch and Stevenson, 2008), benchmarking (Kayser and Peress, 2012), and blind retrospection (Achen and Bartels, 2016).[7]

Finally, the experiments in Section 6 (Exps. 8–11) turn to the use of heuristics – or simplifying information about performance – in the integration-appraisal process. With only minor changes to our basic games, we study individual preferences for different heuristics and the extent to which the availability of objectively "good" performance indicators shapes the use of particular heuristics in the evaluation process.

1.4 Partisan Identity and Experimental Tests of Retrospective Voting

One of the most common questions we received as we presented findings from this project concerns the role of partisan identity in retrospective voting. Given what we know about the effect of partisanship on political behavior, should that variable not play an explicit role in our otherwise abstract framework? Put differently, shouldn't we abandon the factory worker in favor of a more politically "realistic" design? Our answer – which is no – goes to the heart of our theoretical and empirical approach. While Sections 2 and 3 elaborate our understanding of these issues in detail, given the centrality of partisan social identity to contemporary scholarship, we briefly summarize our perspective here.

---

[7] Our discussion of Experiments 5–9 reproduces parts of Hart and Matthews (2022).

The motivation for this Element is theory-testing: to evaluate and advance models of retrospective voting. We aim to generalize from the behaviors we observe in the experiments to the theories themselves and not, for example, to the incumbent's vote share in a specific election or under specific economic conditions. Introducing variables extraneous to the models we test defeats the purpose of experimentation and, for theory-testing endeavors, limits generalizability. As we argue in Section 2, efforts to increase the "mundane realism" of experimental treatments and settings does not confer external validity on theory-testing experiments (see also McDermott, 2002; Druckman, 2022). Similarly, the omission of concrete realities beyond the scope of the theories being tested does not threaten external validity. When the goal is theoretical rather than statistical generalization, an experiment is externally valid "if it is an instance of the theory it tests and neither adds nor subtracts anything from the theory" (Zelditch, 2007, p. 96). This approach, though not novel (e.g., Lupia and McCubbins, 1998), highlights a major point of departure from much contemporary thinking in experimental political science about generalizability.

Consider the possibility that partisanship moderates the retrospective vote. Would assigning a salient social identity to the incumbent "workers" in our experiments moderate responses to their performance? Probably so. For instance, Brutger et al. (2022) find that adding details and context to experimental settings may dampen treatment effects. But so too, we think, would presenting the instructions – to our English-speaking respondents – in Dutch. Keeping in mind that neither variable is an essential element of models of retrospective voting, would introducing these extraneous moderators increase our leverage over the theories we test? No. We would join the queue of observational and experimental studies that we have already suggested fail to identify and effectively explore the integration-appraisal task. To be sure, theoretical claims regarding party identification's impact on how voters seek out, integrate, and appraise performance information are well worth testing. Yet these processes are extraneous to the models we test, and exploratory mediation analysis must play second fiddle to foundational tests of retrospection. After all, we have seventy-odd years of empirical study and few clear insights into how, and how well, voters manage the central task of retrospective voting.

1.5 Preview of Findings

Our studies reveal a retrospective voter who can – and often does – make sensible use of the performance information they encounter. Participants in our experiments reward and punish incumbents in accordance with their productivity and do so without the aid of simplifying summaries and evaluative interpretations.

Confronted with the problem of interdependence, our participants avail of salient comparisons, or benchmarks, in a way that clarifies their incumbent's unique contribution to performance. This tendency to rely on benchmarks is surprisingly robust – and it sometimes leads the participants in our studies astray. We also find the integration and appraisal process subject to distortions (or biases) that are common in other domains of human decision-making. Overall, however, the retrospective voter implied by our results processes information in a way that ably, if not always optimally, identifies competent incumbents.

Furthermore, the research in this Element identifies new – and underexamined – questions for retrospective voting scholars. Perhaps most notably, a host of findings highlight the role of informational context in the formation of performance evaluations; among other things, these results point to the consequences of most past experimentalists' decisions to simplify the appraisal process by suggesting evaluative interpretations as part of their experimental treatments. We also study the impact of dimensions of performance – its variability and negativity – that have received scant attention in existing experimental literature: Our results here are mixed, which only underlines the need for much more work in these areas. Relatedly, we encounter unexpected complexity at the core of the integration-appraisal process, involving the sequence in which these two fundamental tasks unfold; our analysis suggests that, for work on certain questions, this is a complexity that researchers cannot ignore.

Ultimately, we hope to shed light on the normative significance of one of the most widely observed regularities in voting behavior. What do we learn about democratic accountability when we observe, for example, a voter sanctioning an incumbent in the midst of an economic recession? What about when we observe the voter failing to do so? The central premise of this Element is that the virtues of retrospective voting – its promise for motivating responsive government – only hold to the extent that the judgments voters' register on Election Day reflect a sensible integration and appraisal of their incumbent's performance. While we cannot be sure that the tendencies we observe in our experiments obtain in real-world elections, our results show that voters are at least capable of forming and acting upon more reliable and more discerning judgments than some prominent models of retrospective voting suggest. For democrats, this is an encouraging conclusion.

2 The Case for Abstract Experimental Design

What can we learn from abstract laboratory or survey experiments like the ones we present in this Element? Early experiments in the social sciences abstracted away from the complexities of the real world, creating carefully controlled "synthetic" settings ideal for testing the predictions of theory. Experiments in this tradition remain common but concerns about the unrealism of the environments they create loom large. The conventional view is that our capacity to generalize from an experimental setting depends on its "mundane realism," or the parallelism between the real world and the experimental analogue.[8] As such, randomized evaluations – experiments conducted in the field and with the treatment and outcome of interest – increasingly set the standard for experimental design (e.g., Angrist and Pischke, 2015, p. 1). Findley et al. (2021), for example, claim that "whereas [randomized evaluations] generally have high mundane realism, some – but not all! – laboratory and survey experiments do not and thus provide a poor basis for external validity inferences" (p. 371).

We argue that concerns about abstraction in experimental design – the creation of hypothetical, minimalistic, and/or largely acontextual lab or survey "worlds" – are misplaced. The confusion stems from a presumption that all experimental research shares a common epistemic aim. In this section, we make a simple but critical distinction between "impact-estimating" and "theory-testing" inquiry. This is not a novel typology,[9] but we build on prior work by showing how and why these differences motivate distinct approaches to abstraction versus realism in experimental design. We argue that concerns about mundane realism are appropriate for impact-estimating studies, where the target of generalization is itself complex and context-bound. Theory-testing or model-driven efforts, in contrast, should pursue idealized and largely acontextual designs: They should strive to create "synthetic" worlds that mirror the simplified worlds of the theories under scrutiny. Synthetic experiments that seek to incorporate elements of mundane realism are no more externally valid a priori than more abstract alternatives; they simply serve different epistemic ends. If anything, we may be concerned about a lack of abstraction, not of mundane realism, in behavioral experiments.

2.1 External Validity and the Appeal of Randomized Evaluations

The hallmark of experimental methodology is the random assignment of units to different values of treatment. Randomization ensures that the allocation of units to treatment or comparison groups is independent of any factor that might affect

---

[8] Mutz (2011), for example, differentiates mundane realism – the similarity between the study setting and the setting encountered in the real world – from experimental or psychological realism – the extent to which subjects attend to, or take as real, the experimental task.

[9] In political science, see especially Druckman (2022). Similar arguments are found in economics (e.g., Roth, 1995), sociology (e.g., Lucas, 2003), psychology (e.g., Mook, 1983), and philosophy of science (e.g. Pozzoni and Kaidesoja, 2021). Alternatively, see Guala (2005) or Banerjee (2005).

the outcome. Consequently, the measured response of a comparison group is equivalent in expectation to the response of those assigned to treatment had they been assigned instead to a comparison. This promise of a credible counterfactual elevated experiments to the "gold standard" of causal identification across the social and medical sciences.

Yet persistent concerns about generalizability temper the propagation of experimental methods. Many early social science experiments took place in carefully controlled labs – synthetic worlds with few concrete features (e.g., Smith 1962; Fiorina and Plott 1978). A kind of localism emerged in response to the obvious disjuncture between the real world and the artificial laboratory or survey analogue. At the extreme end, Latour (1984) posits that experimental findings are bound to the environment from which they emerge; findings may travel from lab to lab but not beyond. Guala (2005, p. 7) outlines a more typical position, arguing that "it is difficult to extend experimental results to real-world circumstances unless we are able to shape the experiment and the real world so as to resemble each other."

Randomized evaluations – also field experiments or randomized control trials – sought to confront the problem of generality by erasing the laboratory/field distinction wherever possible.[10] Attempting to mimic the success of clinical trials in medicine (Banerjee and Duflo, 2011, p. 8), randomized evaluations evaluate impact by administering the treatment of interest to a population of interest in the context of interest. Cohen and Dupas (2010), for example, randomized the price at which Kenyan health clinics sold insecticide-treated bed nets to pregnant women and then monitored usage. Rather than relying on synthetic laboratory or survey analogues, the design offers a direct assessment of the target policy (cost-sharing of nets) in the target context.

Like clinical trials, the parallelism of randomized evaluations is meant to "ensure that the results will tell us something useful about the real world, not just some contrived laboratory setting" (Green and Gerber, 2003, p. 94). Randomized evaluations, in this sense, aim to have their cake and eat it too. Experimental methods have claimed pride of place in causal identification since Fisher (1935); now, randomized evaluations claim pride of place in external validity as well. It is notable that Vernon Smith won the 2002 Nobel Prize in economics for his use of laboratory experiments, and, not two decades later, Esther Duflo, Abhijit Banerjee, and Michael Kremer won for their innovations in randomized evaluation methodology, effectively removing the lab from the

---

[10] For guides to randomized evaluations, see Gerber and Green (2012) and Glennerster and Takavarsha (2013). On the history of field experiments in political science, see Green and Gerber (2003).

experiment. Of note, the award letter highlights the external validity of randomized evaluations and their impact on policymaking.

For the many gains of the randomized evaluation revolution, we worry that the lens through which we evaluate experimental research is narrowing. Campbell and Stanley (1963, p. 5) framed generalizability in terms of the other treatments, outcomes, populations, and settings to which experimental findings might extend. The notion we – researchers reliant on synthetic laboratory and survey settings – import from the randomized evaluation framework is more restrictive. Angrist and Pischke (2015) define generality in terms of the "predictive value [of a causal estimate] for times, places, and people beyond those represented in the study" (p. 114). This takes the treatment and outcome measures as fixed, and it ignores the possibility of generalization beyond the impact estimate itself. It reduces an encompassing notion of general knowledge to a narrow question of predictive capacity. This, in turn, makes mundane realism a necessary condition for this type of generalization.[11]

Against this benchmark, it is doubtful that survey and laboratory experiments that abstract away from the treatments, outcomes, or settings of interest can be a source of general knowledge. Mutz (2011) notes that "field experiments are routinely claimed to be more generalizable simply because they are field experiments" (p. 135). Further, whenever abstraction seems unavoidable, researchers feel obliged to seek the trappings of mundane realism to help compensate. We craft survey experimental vignettes to mimic the style and appearance of newspaper articles (e.g., Hart and Middleton, 2014) or add couches to the laboratory to mimic participants' living rooms (Iyengar and Kinder, 1987). In most cases, these steps toward realism are taken without empirical or theoretical grounding, and they may or may not enhance external validity.[12] They may simply reflect a convention that any effort at mundane realism is a step in the right direction. In the rest of this section, we argue that the convention is misguided and that the pursuit of mundane realism outside the context of impact evaluation does not establish, and may in fact limit, external validity.

---

[11] We might assume that Cohen and Dupas's (2010) randomized evaluation, for example, improves inferences about their program's impact on net usage in Kenya. It is unclear, however, if its realism should also improve predictions about alternative cost-sharing programs with other goods, other outcome measures, or in other contexts.

[12] See especially Brutger et al. (2022) for a practical guide to the impact of decisions about abstraction versus specificity in experimental design. While the implicit target here is impact-estimating generalization, a key takeaway is that some design decisions are more consequential than others.

2.2 On Generalization

Before differentiating impact-estimating and theory-testing inquiry, we offer brief clarifying comments on generalization.[13] The first is that establishing generality is necessarily inductive. We cannot directly (or fully) observe the generality of an experimental finding. Through repeated evaluation, we may see that a result extends to other labs, settings, units, treatments, or outcome measures. Even here, generalizability is never assured, and the realism or unrealism of the evaluation neither establishes nor moderates its success (Rodrik, 2008). Banerjee (2020), for example, offers an important commentary on inductive reasoning as the basis for generalization in randomized evaluation methodology, noting that "the idea is to implement the same concept in multiple locations to build confidence in its impact (or to discover that it only works in certain circumstances)" (p. 1938).

How can we identify the cases to which an experimental result might and might not extend? Orr et al. (2019, p. 979) suggest that the proliferation of randomized evaluations offers policymakers a "wealth of evidence describing *what* works, but not necessarily *where*." Our second point, then, is that out-of-study generalization requires assumptions about the causal processes at work and their interplay with context. Again, this is true independent of the mode of evaluation and the degree of parallelism sought. For example, we might use a randomized evaluation to establish that an intervention works. To then suggest that the findings extend to site A but not B or message C but not D requires a set of priors about how and why the intervention works and how that interacts with the complex realities of A and B or C and D. The rub is that uncertainty about those priors is often the motivation for the study. Consider that Cohen and Dupas's (2010) findings in Kenya were inconsistent with a similar cost-sharing randomized evaluation in Zambia (Ashraf et al., 2010). Rather than highlight the broad generality of their findings, Cohen and Dupas (2010) speculate about the unique differences between the study sites and treatments, and the potential interactions between them.

None of this is meant to suggest that generalization is folly. Rather, we aim to highlight that neither the method of evaluation nor the pursuit of mundane realism confers generalizability on an experiment. Realism may help establish an effect within a specific domain but it does not establish that the domain of the effect is universal (or even broad). In this sense, mundane realism might combat the problem of reality – improving estimates of the impact of an intervention in

---

[13] For extended discussions of external validity in the philosophy of science, see Cartwright (2007) and Guala (2005). For applied overviews, see especially Mutz (2011, chap. 8) and Druckman (2022, chap. 3).

the target context – but cannot overcome the problem of generality. Banerjee and Duflo (e.g., Banerjee and Duflo, 2009) write frequently about the importance of context and the potential threat of environmental dependence in randomized evaluations. Indeed, some of the most important debates in randomized evaluation methodology address inaccuracy in out-of-study predictions because of effect heterogeneity, spillover, and more (see, e.g., Davis and Mobarak, 2020). With this in mind, we revisit the claim that mundane realism is an appropriate standard for external validity in experimental research writ large.

2.3 Epistemic Goals and Experimental Design

The pursuit of mundane realism follows from an assumption – generally unstated – that experimental research shares a common epistemic aim centered on impact evaluation. We argue, however, that experimentalists who use synthetic designs typically pursue general claims that fall outside the seemingly narrow bounds of their designs. Here, we differentiate between impact-estimating and theory-testing types of inquiry. Critically, we argue that the distinct intellectual goals of these types of inquiry motivate distinct approaches to lab and survey experimental design. The question of generalizability is not about maximizing mundane realism but about matching design to epistemic aim.

Impact-estimating inquiry seeks to generalize from the treatment effect in an experiment to treatment effects beyond the study. This is the motivating force of the randomized evaluation framework, to find out "what works" and "how much" in the study context and then to extend that estimate to similar settings. Critically, the target of generalization is specific and bound by context (i.e., what would be the impact of applying the intervention *exactly here*?). The experimental setting, units, intervention, and outcome, then, should all mimic their respective targets, and mundane realism is essential for generalizing the estimated impact. The reality of the context – and therefore the boundedness of its domain – is a primary source of generality. Externally valid impact estimates, however, are not necessarily broad. Indeed, the scope is tied to the domain of the study setting.

In contrast, theory-testing inquiry pursues the broad tendency claims that define social science models. Rather than asking "how much," experiments in this tradition often seek answers to "how actually" questions (e.g., how *actually* do voters integrate and appraise streams of performance information?). The size of the treatment effect may have little extrinsic value. The behaviors predicted by the model either obtain or do not, and this motivates an update of theoretical priors. The target of generalization in theory-testing experiments is not a specific place but rather the abstract world described by theory. One generalizes from the model emerging from the study to other instantiations of it. Externally valid generalizations, then, are as broad in scope as the model under scrutiny. Yet they lack the "thick" – or contextual/historical – grounding of generalizations from impact-estimating studies. As such, generalizations emerging from theory-testing studies do not speak directly to impact in particular settings – though, of course, they may do so (more or less persuasively) in combination with theoretical propositions that characterize relevant features of the settings in question.

To maximize external validity, a theory-testing experiment must create an instantiation of the theoretical world(s) under scrutiny. Social scientific models are necessarily abstract (minimalistic and acontextual), and experiments that aim to test them must conform to this standard. Critically, the synthesized environment must create the space in which the predicted or contested behaviors could reasonably emerge. In the tradition of many early social science experiments, this requires that the researcher eliminate "all causal factors that may be present in the setting but absent from the theory as it stands" (Pozzoni and Kaidesoja, 2021, p. 19). Mundane realism introduces complicating factors or environmental constraints outside the model and, thus, grounds the study in a specific context. Far from buttressing external validity, these efforts likely limit the scope of generalization. As Plott (1991) argues, "the [abstract] experiment should be judged by the lessons it teaches about the theory and not by its similarity with what nature might have happened to have created" (p. 906).

In a sense, both approaches to inquiry and design are organized around the problem of context, and the limits of each reflect our incomplete understanding of that problem. Theory-testing approaches abstract away from the complications of context, but generalization is limited in practical application by our simplistic rendering of specific settings. Impact-estimating approaches open the door and let the complications of context flow in. In doing so, they offer a look at impact in that context, but generalization is limited by our incomplete understanding of what constitutes similarity across contexts.

As researchers and reviewers, it is critical that we assess experimental research programs in terms of epistemic aim rather than degree of abstraction versus mundane realism. Impact-estimating and theory-testing inquiries ask different questions, seek to apply their answers to different targets, and take different paths to generalization. Mundane realism is critical where the goal is identifying the efficacy of treatment in a specific context or population. Yet realism tethers an experimental result to the context in which it emerged, and this is anathema to the broad aim of theory-testing. As Druckman (2022) notes, "unless one has strongly applied goals to assess an intervention implemented in real time, mundane realism should play little to no role in assessing an experiment" (p. 53). Here, an abstract design is necessary to match the simplified causal processes of the theory.

2.4 Assessing Experimental Designs for Testing Theories

How should we evaluate the potential contributions of theory-testing experiments? On what grounds should we praise or critique efforts to generalize in the theory-testing approach? For the many exceptional guides to randomized evaluations (i.e., Gerber and Green, 2012; Glennerster and Takavarsha, 2013) and the external validity of impact estimates (Findley et al., 2021), we know of little work on best practices in designing abstract experiments for testing theories. Brutger et al. (2022) document the empirical consequences of different types of abstraction versus specificity in experimental vignettes. Mook (1983), Thye (2007), and Cartwright (2007) offer important discussions of the theory-testing versus impact-estimating distinction, and all argue for the use of abstract designs for theory-testing approaches. Druckman (2022) highlights the importance of experimental realism – the extent to which participants attend to, or take seriously, the task at hand – in abstract designs. Mutz (2011, chap. 8) offers a lengthier treatment of external validity across laboratory, field, and population-based survey experiments, highlighting the roles of setting, sampling, and measurement.

We cannot offer a complete guide here, but we build on these contributions in suggesting six considerations for evaluating designs for theory-testing inquiry in lab and survey experiments. The first three concern how the researcher grounds the design and presentation of results:

1. Does the researcher explicitly identify theory-testing and/or model-building as the goal of the study or program?
2. Does the researcher ground efforts at generalization in reference to the theory?
3. Does the researcher clearly and accurately specify the theoretical models – or specific a priori propositions – under study?

Identifying the intent of generalization (1) and grounding conclusions in theory (2) are essential first steps in promoting a more systematic approach to theory-testing experiments. While not directly related to design, we hope these efforts will limit knee-jerk calls for mundane realism and, similarly, discourage researchers using abstract designs from generalizing without direct appeal to theory. Theory-testing studies also require a clear exposition of the theoretical propositions in question (3). After all, the model is the target of generalization. If the researcher fails to properly identify the theoretical target, the reader has no grounds on which to judge the merits or demerits of the design.

We specify three further criteria for evaluating the design itself:

4. Does the experimental environment capture the essential elements of the models and abstract away from or control for inessential and extraneous factors?
5. Does the experimental environment create space for the target behaviors to emerge?
6. Are steps taken to enhance experimental realism without sacrificing the integrity of the abstract environment?

These considerations jointly describe the necessity of creating a diagnostic test of theory. First and foremost, good designs for testing theory are minimalistic: They synthesize an environment that is conceptually similar to the one defined by the competing models (4). Good abstract designs decontextualize the setting and strip away all but the essential elements driving the question or leading to divergent predictions. Such designs attempt to match exactly the simplifying assumptions and stylized environment of the theory under examination. This is true even when it seems clear that the model is incomplete or even incorrect relative to the reality it describes. That said, theoretical parallelism is necessary but not sufficient for generalization. To provide a diagnostic test of theory, the environment must also create space in which the target behaviors can feasibly emerge (5).

It is in relation to criteria 4 and 5 that we expect to see the bulk of criticism leveled at abstract designs for theory-testing. Readers of this Element, for example, might take issue with our translation of the integration-appraisal task to our abstract framework or suggest that the design unduly favors a certain mode of response. We may or may not agree, but the critiques would match our epistemic aim. Such critiques may, therefore, form the basis for revisions to our approach or set the stage for future inquiry (e.g., would the findings change if we add, subtract, or alter factor F, and what would this tell us about the integration-appraisal problem?).

The final consideration (6) highlights the importance of experimental realism and the balance that must be struck between decontextualization and minimalism on the one hand and the synthesis of a valid instantiation of the theory on the other. Participants in abstract studies are typically aware of their involvement in social science research by the nature of, e.g., informed consent. A key implication of our case for abstraction is that we can offer diagnostic tests of theory without transporting participants – literally or figuratively – to the mundane world of politics. It is important, however, that participants understand their task and the synthetic world of the study and that they accept both on their own terms.[14] There is clearly a point at which abstraction in creating an

---

[14] We avoid framing experimental realism in terms of participants' level of attention or seriousness as we do not believe these are broadly necessary.

artificial world goes too far: Either it fails to represent an instantiation of the model (lacking "construct validity" and violating criterion 4) or it provides participants with too little information or structure to perform the task in earnest (violating criterion 6). Participants may accept as genuine a researcher's request to evaluate hypothetical candidates for a hypothetical election. They may, however, reject the task upon discovering the "hypothetical" candidates are named Ronald Plump and Celery Hinton. In the context of our retrospective voting "games," it seems necessary that participants believe they are playing a legitimate decision-making game, that they have the power to do well or poorly, and that the incentive structure is credible.

A single experiment may not be able to satisfy all concerns. It is important to remember, then, that generalization is a process, even in the theory-testing context. We should evaluate the external validity of a research program rather than that of an individual experiment. Even within the context of this Element, the importance of understanding a given experiment as part of an extended series of investigations is manifest. For example, as we discuss in Section 5, concerns that Experiment 5 may not have created space for certain behaviors (specifically, blind retrospection and rational discounting) motivated additional experiments (Exps. 6–9) seeking in different ways to open those doors.

2.5 Summary

What can we learn from laboratory and survey experiments that abstract away from the treatments, outcomes, or settings of ultimate interest? We made a positive case in this section that abstract designs are important sources of generalizable knowledge and that the pursuit of mundane realism may limit external validity. Critical to this argument is the distinction between what we have called impact-estimating and theory-testing inquiry. We argued that these approaches ask different questions, seek different answers, and aim to generalize to different targets. In turn, these approaches should motivate distinct experimental designs. Against generic calls to maximize mundane realism, we argue that generalization from theory-testing experiments requires abstract designs that mimic the simplified worlds of the theories they test.

3 Experimental Framework

We stressed in Section 2 that experimental designs should be evaluated in terms of their alignment with the researcher's epistemic aims, emphasizing that designs for impact-estimating and theory-testing inquiry ought to be judged according to different standards. In this Element, our goal is to provide new tests of retrospective voting theory – to identify general tendencies concerning voters' evaluation of incumbents' past performance and the application of these evaluations to the decision of whether to reappoint or replace a current incumbent.

In designing our experimental framework, two challenges loom large. First, as explained in Section 1, we aim not to short-circuit the integration-appraisal task at the heart of retrospective voting theory. We need a design, that is, that surfaces what we have called the streaming quality of performance information and that does not significantly encroach on participants' autonomy in forming appraisals of the performance that they observe. Second, we require a framework that is sufficiently general and flexible that it can incorporate variations allowing us to specify clear tests of diverse propositions regarding retrospective voting. While flexibility in the design is not a source of internal or external validity in any specific study, it maximizes the comparability of results across our numerous and varied experimental designs. In this section, we describe and evaluate our response to these two design challenges, summarize details of our samples and approach to preregistration, and present evidence regarding participant engagement in our studies.

3.1 Outlining the Framework

3.1.1 The Baseline Game

While the empirical work in this Element consists of eleven separate experiments, each can be understood as a variation on a single design, what we call the "baseline game."[15] As noted in Section 1, Huber et al.'s (2012) incentivized experimental game provides the foundation of our framework. Our key departure from their design is that we change the metaphor: Rather than observing an abstract allocator delivering tokens, participants in our studies supervise a worker (or workers) producing "units" in a factory. The principal virtue of the worker metaphor is that we can draw on stereotyped knowledge of workers and factories to simplify exposition of the features of our experimental environments. Given the objectives of some of our experiments, this is a considerable advantage. For instance, for reasons we explain in Sections 5 and 6, some of our experiments involve the late arrival or unexpected early departure of workers (Exps. 5–9); another experiment involves workers operating machines with different efficiency characteristics (Exp. 11). These features are easily introduced within the worker metaphor; doing so in the context of the allocator metaphor would add complexity (and perhaps arbitrariness) to the experimental

---

[15] We use the term "game" loosely, inasmuch as our experiments do not involve interdependent choice.

environment without the support of culturally available tropes relating to factory production.

The baseline game – which, like all our experiments, we field online – asks the participant to serve as a factory supervisor overseeing the performance of an employee. The supervisor's duty is to monitor the worker's output over an initial period of sixteen "weeks" and then decide whether to reappoint or replace the employee. A reappointed employee continues working for another sixteen weeks, otherwise a replacement worker is brought in for the final term. The game ends after thirty-two weeks with the reported tally of "units" produced. To motivate participants to choose workers who maximize worker performance, we award a cash bonus proportional to total factory output over the full thirty-two weeks of the game.

The game begins with a short battery of demographic questions and an attention screen.[16] Next, we present the game instructions and introduce the basic logic of the experimental task, what we describe as the "rules of the game."[17] We inform participants that they are to serve as a factory supervisor "in charge of evaluating employee performance" and will observe a new worker's performance over a trial period of sixteen weeks. After this initial period, they will decide whether to extend the incumbent worker's contract, and the instructions emphasize that the goal is to choose workers who produce the most units. Importantly, we specify how worker performance is linked to the participant's material interests: that they will earn a $1 bonus for every 60,000 units the worker produces.

We then introduce the participant's employee – the incumbent, styled "Worker A" in the instructions – and the parameters of expected worker performance. We explain that the worker is fully trained but that it is not yet clear how the worker will perform on the job. Couched in nontechnical language about factory records, we explain that a worker's (expected) average production, or type, is a random draw from a uniform distribution ranging from 950 to 1,450 units per week ($\mu_w \sim U(950,1450)$). We also indicate that "a worker's output varies each week for reasons beyond their control" and – again using nontechnical language – that weekly production tends to follow a normal distribution centered around the worker's expected average ($W_t \sim N(\mu_w, 250)$). Finally, we note that the parameters of worker performance do not change over time.[18] Importantly, the information about worker

---

[16] We removed 16 percent of potential respondents for failing the attention screen.

[17] The instructions are presented over two screens. Participants cannot advance screens in fewer than ten seconds. They can also opt to review the instructions as quickly or slowly as they like.

[18] This instruction is intended to discourage participants from inferring that their worker improves through experience, which may promote an incumbency bias (but see Section 4).

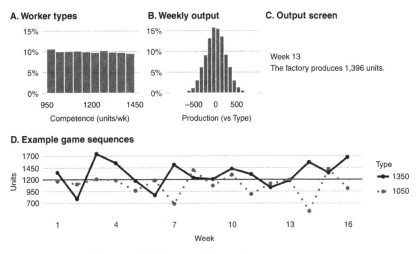

Figure 1 Worker profiles and game sequence

performance is presented such that it applies both to the incumbent worker and to any potential replacements. Figure 1(A)–(B) summarizes the realized parameters of worker performance.

Next, participants are exposed to sixteen weeks of performance. Each week's performance report appears on a separate screen (Figure 1(C)). Participants must click a button to advance to the next week's report and, thus, can spend as much (or as little) time as they wish considering the performance information. After week 8, participants are reminded that they "will need to decide after week 16" whether to retain or replace their incumbent. The reminder exists to align this feature of the design with Experiments 5 to 9, which interrupt the stream of performance information and, among other things, provide a similar reminder. Presumably, the reminder increases attention and the disposition to evaluate performance, relative to what it would be in the absence of the reminder. For reference, Figure 1(D) shows the revealed streams for incumbent workers of two underlying types chosen at random from the game parameters.

After week 16, participants decide whether to retain or replace their incumbent. Our principal dependent variable throughout this Element, the measure asks the participant, "Would you like to extend Worker A's contract or hire a new worker?" We advise participants that, if they choose to replace their incumbent, a new worker will transfer in from elsewhere in the factory. We remind the subject that the replacement's type is unknown but follows the same distribution of worker types. We also note that a replaced incumbent would "return to their prior department" (to mitigate any worries participants may have about their worker's fate).

Once participants render their decisions, the experiment concludes with two questions designed to capture comprehension of the game instructions (see Section 3.3) and a report of the final sixteen weeks of factory production (including the participant's implied cash bonus). If the incumbent worker is retained, the last sixteen weeks are simply another set of draws from the normal distribution centered on the incumbent's type. If the incumbent is replaced, the draws are from a distribution centered on the new worker's type (which, as indicated, is drawn from the same uniform distribution).

This baseline framework is flexible enough to incorporate features that permit tests of a wide range of retrospective voting expectations. Some modifications can be introduced with no – or almost no – changes to the text of the instructions. In Experiment 2, for instance, we manipulate the variance of weekly performance; conversely, Experiment 4 holds constant the incumbent's type and weekly performances but manipulates the weekly sequence. These variations would be completely imperceptible to someone who happened (unlike our participants) to complete more than one of these experiments. We can also, without modifying the game instructions, introduce opportunities to acquire performance information (as in Exps. 8 and 10) or manipulate exposure to such information (as in Exp. 9). Perhaps the most significant variation on the baseline game involves exposure to streams of performance information involving more than one worker (Exps. 5–9 and 11). Even here, however, modifications to the instructions are slight and, except for Experiment 11, we expose participants to just one stream of performance information at a time.[19]

3.1.2 Recruitment and Sample

We recruited samples of US adults to participate in our studies, using Amazon. com's Mechanical Turk web services.[20] From summer 2018 through spring 2022, 9,157 individuals attempted our experimental games. We offered a baseline payment of $0.30 ($0.40 in 2022), along with the chance to earn a bonus. Bonuses averaged $0.67 across all studies. To mitigate temporal bias in the available worker pool (Casey et al., 2017), we automated calls for batches of

---

[19] One limitation of our design is that it does not incorporate the possibility that voters may respond to incumbent performance with abstention. While this dynamic has not been central to empirical work on retrospective voting (Gomez and Hansford, 2015), it could, in principle, be incorporated into our experimental framework by, for example, allowing participants to delegate their supervisory authority to others of uncertain quality. We thank Eline de Rooij for highlighting the significance of this possibility.

[20] We programmed the game in Qualtrics. Contact the authors for the JavaScript routines. All studies presented in this Element were conducted in compliance with relevant laws in the United States and Canada and were approved by the Institutional Review Board at American University or the Interdisciplinary Committee on Ethics in Human Research at Memorial University.

9 to 100 respondents at fixed intervals, typically over multiple days. Based on self-reports, the subject pool was 44 percent female and 70 percent white with a median age of 30–39 years. The 7,309 who completed the experiments did so in about six minutes on average.

3.1.3 Preregistration and Replication

We preregistered designs and analysis plans for Experiments 1–4 and 7–11 using the Open Science Framework (osf.io). We perform and report all preregistered analyses.[21] While most of our analyses are preregistered, we also present unplanned analyses. With one exception,[22] the principal hypotheses examined in each study are subjected to one or more preregistered experimental tests.

The Online Appendix to this Element includes further information that may be of interest to readers.[23] This includes links to replication data and all preregistrations, the full text of study rules and questions, details on sample demographics, randomization checks, estimates of alternative model specifications, and more.

3.2 Evaluating the Approach

In Section 2, we proposed six questions for evaluating theory-testing experimental research. The first three of these questions relate to the researcher's success in articulating their intended generalization – in identifying theory-testing generalization as their epistemic goal, specifying the theoretical model in relation to which the generalization is to be made, and grounding generalization with reference to that model. We leave it to the reader to decide whether, reflecting on the whole of this Element, our approach succeeds or fails by these criteria. We do wish, however, to offer some arguments in relation to the design-oriented evaluative considerations raised in Section 2.

Does the experimental environment capture the essential elements of the models and abstract away from or control for inessential and extraneous factors? We argue in Section 1 that at the core of retrospective voting theory is the idea that the decision to reelect or replace an incumbent is affected by voters' evaluations of the state of the world. We also emphasize that the formation of these evaluations requires the voter to integrate a stream of

---

[21] These are identified by footnotes containing links to the registrations. Note that some preregistration documents refer to performance voting, rather than retrospective voting. We regard these terms as equivalent.

[22] We did not preregister, in relation to Experiment 2, the expectation that the variability of worker performance would negatively affect worker retention, on average.

[23] The Online Appendix is available at https://www.cambridge.org/HartMatthewsSupplementary Materials.

information relevant to performance into a summary impression that must, in turn, be appraised. In capturing these essential features of retrospective voting, we suggest our design very clearly succeeds. Most fundamentally, the design requires participants to "vote" for or against an incumbent whose performance in "office" is linked to the "state of the world." A vote against the incumbent, furthermore, results in a replacement taking office whose performance the voter has not had a similar opportunity to observe – a fundamental information asymmetry between incumbents and challengers that has been noted since Downs (1957). As we have emphasized, a critical feature of our design is that the subject confronts a stream of variable performance information that they must somehow integrate and appraise. Importantly, our design provides a basis for performance appraisal. Specifically, the game instructions explain the link between worker performance and the participant's interests – i.e., that more production means a higher payout at the end of the game. This feature aligns the design with the simplest, if unstated, premise of retrospective voting theory: that voters have preferences over different states of the world.

If our design includes the necessary features of the retrospective voting model, we also argue that it *excludes* those features that are unnecessary (though what is necessary varies by study to some degree). The experimental setting is rather austere, providing only information regarding workers' weekly performance and just as much instructional information as required to clarify how alternative "vote" decisions link to the participant's interests. Note that the desire to exclude extraneous factors from the experimental setting motivates, in part, our decision not to place the game in an explicitly political context. Even if such a design involved a hypothetical situation referring only to fictional politicians and polities, we fear participants may, nonetheless, be influenced by analogies between the experimental setting and real-world politics. For instance, our American participants may naturally associate a hypothetical "incumbent executive officeholder" with the sitting president, potentially introducing the influence of a host of strong attitudes and beliefs. While the factory metaphor may invite associations to real-world factories among some participants, our assumption is that the implicated attitudes would be weaker, on average, than those an explicitly political metaphor would raise.

Does the study environment create space for the target behaviors or tendencies to emerge? If we have succeeded in eliminating extraneous factors from the design, then we are some distance toward creating space for retrospective voting to emerge. At the same time, our design aims to engender performance-voting effects that can be precisely estimated. The informational austerity of the design, by eliminating alternative influences on behavior, should reduce the residual variance in worker retention decisions and, furthermore, concentrate attention on the decision criterion of theoretical interest, i.e., worker perform-ance. Further, while the stream of performance information is noisy, incorporat-ing the over-time variation we regard as inherent in the challenge of retrospective voting, it nonetheless provides a strong signal of incumbent quality. As such, performance-oriented voters' likelihood of reappointing their workers ought to vary considerably across the range of worker types observed in the experiment.

Are steps taken to enhance experimental realism without sacrificing the integrity of the abstract environment? The use of incentives linked to factory production is our main strategy to promote participants' serious engagement with the experimental task. While the average payout is modest, roughly two-thirds of the average payout reflects the participant's success in maximizing factory production through their worker-retention decisions. We also suspect that the use of the culturally familiar factory metaphor may encourage accept-ance of the task, relative to less-familiar metaphors (which may be less well understood) or purely researcher-generated hypothetical worlds (which may feel especially arbitrary or trivial).

3.3 Participant Engagement

We conclude this section with a first look at our data. While these analyses do not constitute informative tests of retrospective voting theory, they do speak to the nature of participant engagement with our experiments and, thus, provide evidence relevant to the evaluation of our design.

First, as noted, all experiments concluded with two questions designed to gauge comprehension of the game instructions. The questions focus on the distributional parameters of worker performance, particularly comprehension of the uniform distribution of worker types and the normal distribution of workers' weekly performance (correct answers in italics):

> If you replace a worker who averaged 1,200 units per week, is the new hire more likely to average 1,000 or 1,400 units per week? (1,000 is more likely; 1,400 is more likely; *1,000 and 1,400 are equally likely*; Don't know)

> If a worker averages 1,100 units per week, are they more likely to produce 1,300 or 1,500 units next week? (*1,300 is more likely*; 1,500 is more likely; 1,300 and 1,500 are equally likely; Don't know)

We regard correct responses to these items as an index of overall attention to and comprehension of the experimental task. (Note that we do not exclude anyone from our analyses on the basis of comprehension.) Figure 2(A) plots the distribution of correct responses. Importantly, participants seem largely to have understood the game design: Across all studies, 78 percent answered at least one of the questions correctly and about one-third (32 percent) answered

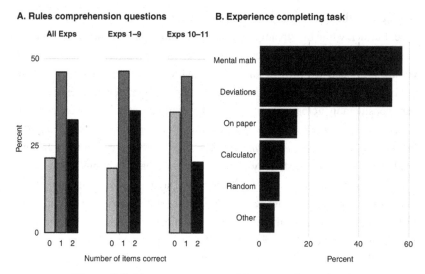

Figure 2 Subject engagement with game rules and task

both correctly. We also note that the rate of correct responses drops considerably in Experiments 10 and 11. These studies are unique insofar as we remove from the instructions any reference to the uniform distribution of worker type (see Section 6). Note that without this information the rate of participants failing to answer either question correctly nearly doubles.

Second, Experiments 2 and 3 included a question designed to query participants' subjective experience of completing the experimental game:

> Finally, we'd like to know a little about how you played the game. Did you apply any of the following techniques as you played the game? You may indicate as many or as few techniques as you like.
>
> There is no correct answer to this question and, remember, your response will not affect your earnings.

- Recorded the worker's weekly production (e.g., on a sheet of paper)
- Used a calculator or spreadsheet
- Used "mental math"
- Took note of production numbers that were far above or below the factory average of 1,200
- Chose randomly (e.g., by flipping a coin)
- Used some other technique

While certain responses speak directly to the nature of participants' integration and appraisal strategies (particularly the options of "chose randomly" and "took note of production numbers . . ."), we are skeptical of participants' ability, in general, to provide veridical accounts of their cognitive processes. Rather, the primary value of these data lies in the insight they provide regarding participants' level of engagement with the experimental task.

Figure 2(B) shows that only a small proportion indicated that they chose randomly, an option that would suggest a failure to accept the experimental task on its own terms. Conversely, more than half of participants indicated either that they "used mental math" or that they "took note" of production values far from the factory mean. Indeed, nearly 85 percent of participants indicated they applied one or both "techniques" as they completed the experiment. We also note that only a small share of participants went as far as to "record" weekly performance values, and even fewer "used a calculator or spreadsheet" to aid their decision-making. As both techniques suggest a level of engagement beyond that assumed by retrospective voting theory, we take these findings as reassuring.

4 Retrospective Voting: Tests of Integration and Appraisal

We argue that the task of integrating and appraising a stream of variable performance information is central to the logic of retrospective voting and that almost all existing experimental tests of retrospective voting short-circuit this process by design. As such, we have very limited experimental evidence speaking to the core information-processing challenge of retrospective voting. In this section, we expand the relevant experimental evidence base considerably.

With Experiment 1, we aim to provide a clean test of retrospective voting – of the proposition that voters can integrate over a stream of variable performance, form an appraisal thereof, and apply that appraisal to the decision of whether to retain or replace an incumbent. Experiment 2 focuses on a feature of performance that is invisible in the typical retrospective voting experiment: the variability of performance over time. Experiment 3 presents a test of the well-known negativity bias – the tendency for negative information to attract more attention, and ultimately carry more evaluative weight, than positive information. Lastly, Experiment 4 focuses on bias in the temporal dimension, examining whether voters apply undue weight to either early performance ("primacy bias") or late performance ("recency bias").

4.1 Experiment 1: Can Voters Integrate and Appraise Performance?

4.1.1 Design and Expectations

We provide a simple test of retrospective voting that does not spare experimental participants the work of integration and appraisal. In the context of the baseline game, described in Section 3.1.1, standard retrospective voting theory implies a positive relationship between worker performance and retention.[24] Our design motivates retrospective voting by specifying a payout structure that creates an incentive for participants to maximize worker output. We assume that appraisals of incumbent performance will generally be informed by the distribution of worker types outlined in the game instructions. As Huber et al. (2012) explain, this feature of the game implies an optimal strategy for risk-neutral participants: retain incumbents above the distribution's average (i.e., 1,200 units) and replace those below the distribution's average. While we are doubtful that many participants will consciously apply exactly this strategy, we are optimistic that a large subset will approach it intuitively. For instance, participants may reward (punish) incumbents whose performance nears the top (bottom) of the range of worker types.

4.1.2 Results

A total of 248 participants provided complete responses in Experiment 1. Figure 3(A) shows for reference the distribution of worker types, both assigned and revealed. Figure 3(C) presents linear regression estimates of the impact of average performance (scaled in 100s of units) on the decision to reappoint the incumbent worker. Given the binary dependent variable, this is a linear probability model; thus, we can interpret the slope coefficient as the change in the probability of reappointing the incumbent associated with a 100-unit increase in the incumbent's weekly average. Consistent with our expectations, this coefficient estimate is positive: On average, an increase of 100 units raises the probability of retention by 11 points ($p < 0.001$). Note also that this finding highlights the impact of our core manipulation throughout this Element: Varying the incumbent's underlying type changes how respondents see the value of reappointing the incumbent.

Figure 3(B) plots this relationship, along with an overlay of a nonparametric estimate of the relationship, using locally weighted scatterplot smoothing (LOWESS). The comparison suggests that the linear function is a reasonable approximation of the relationship (though perhaps a little less so for the worst-performing workers). Notably, while this functional form implies a sensible relationship between performance and retention, it is far from consistent with perfectly rational retrospective voting. As explained in Section 4.1.1, risk-neutral participants ought to retain (replace) incumbents above (below) the

---

[24] We assume throughout that voters know, at least to an approximation, what's good for them and that they can make use of available information to act in ways that are at least broadly consistent with their interests. We preregistered expectations for Experiment 1: https://doi.org/10.17605/OSF.IO/UJ9BW.

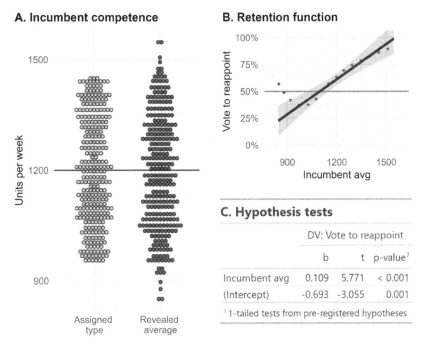

Figure 3 Integrating and appraising performance, Experiment 1

distribution's average of 1,200 units. Further, when production equals 1,200 units, participants should be indifferent between retention and replacement, perhaps tossing a fair coin to decide whether to retain their worker. This implies an (approximate) step function, with all below-average workers replaced, all above-average workers retained, and perfectly average workers retained at a rate of 0.5. Instead, our participants' tendency to discriminate between above- and below-average workers is much sharper as workers approach the extremes of the range of worker performance, where, presumably, distinctions in worker quality are most obvious.

Figure 3 also reveals a significant incumbency bias. Given strategically optimal behavior, the retention rate at 1,200 units would equal 50 percent. However, whether considering the parametric or nonparametric estimate, Figure 3(B) clearly shows that "average" incumbents have a much better than even chance of retention: The regression estimate implies that workers are retained with a probability of 0.61 (95% CI = [0.55,0.67]) when worker production averages 1,200 units.

Overall, the results are consistent with the image of a satisficing retrospective voter. Of special importance given questions in the literature about the capacity of voters to manage the integration-appraisal task, retention decisions in

Experiment 1 are sensibly, and rather strongly, related to worker performance. This is true even with the provision of raw performance outcomes rather than pre-integrated and/or pre-appraised performance summaries. At the same time, the nature of the performance–retention relationship suggests a voter with a less-than-perfect ability to integrate over a stream of performance information and who may be biased in favor of the status quo.

4.2 Experiment 2: Does Performance Variability Matter?

4.2.1 Design and Expectations

The variability of performance – an inherent feature of a stream of performance information, even if competence does *not* vary – introduces a second potential dimension to the evaluation of performance. Voters who observe the unfolding of performance over time can, in addition to the level of performance, take account of whether incumbents deliver consistent, predictable results.

We consider the impact of performance variability with a simple development on the baseline game: In addition to randomly assigning the worker's underlying type, we also randomize the variability of weekly output. In one condition, the expected standard deviation of the worker's weekly output is 250 units, as it is for nearly all the hypothetical workers in our studies, including Experiment 1. In the other, "low-variance" condition, the expected standard deviation of the worker's output is much lower, just 100 units, though still sufficiently variable that integration of performance information is nontrivial.

Performance variability may be used differently by voters depending on their underlying objective in evaluating performance. Risk-averse voters seeking to motivate good performance may sanction inconsistent performers for the unpredictability they impart to the social world (Quinn and Woolley, 2001). Similarly, risk-averse voters who evaluate performance with a view to selecting high-quality incumbents may prefer consistent performers for the same reason – i.e., they prefer predictability – or because consistent performers are seen as revealing more certain information about their underlying quality.

These arguments imply a negative relationship between the variability of worker performance and worker retention.[25] At the same time, variability may interact with the level of performance. In the selection model, the weight of average worker performance in retention decisions may be proportional to the certainty of that estimate. Alternatively, performance variability may complicate the integration of performance information, introducing random error

---

[25] This expectation is registered here: https://doi.org/10.17605/OSF.IO/KQ47M.

into overall impressions that systematically weakens the link between worker performance and retention.

4.2.2 Results

Four hundred and three participants completed Experiment 2. Figure 4(A) compares the retention function for incumbent workers among participants assigned to the high-variance (blue/dark shading) and low-variance (yellow/ light shading) conditions. Figure 4(C) presents regression estimates of this interactive model. Again, we express worker performance in 100s of units for ease of interpretation.

The effect of performance in the "high-variance" condition – which replicates the design of Experiment 1 – is sizable and statistically significant. The effect of a 100-unit increase in performance in this condition is, on its face, slightly smaller than that in Experiment 1, roughly a 7-point increase in the probability of retention ($p < 0.001$).[26] Contrary to our expectations, the effect of performance is not significantly different in the low-variance condition: The interaction between worker performance and condition is small and statistically insignificant ($p = 0.777$, 1-tailed). Likewise, there is no "main effect" of variability: While the coefficient on the low-variance condition is sizable, it applies to a level of performance – zero units – well below the range observed in

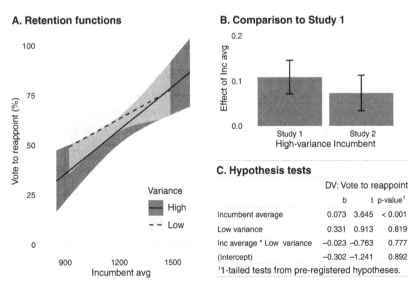

Figure 4 Null effect of incumbent performance variability, Experiment 2

---

[26] The difference between experiments is not statistically significant ($p = 0.195$).

the experiment. Across the observed range of performance there is no significant difference in retention between the low- and high-variance conditions.

The results of Experiment 2 suggest that performance variability does not dampen the weight participants attach to worker performance or limit participants' ability to form impressions of performance. Neither does variability exert an independent influence on retention. At least over the range examined here, incumbent performance variability is not an important dimension of performance evaluation.

4.3 Experiment 3: Is Bad Performance Punished Asymmetrically?

4.3.1 Design and Expectations

A vast literature in psychology finds that negatively appraised information is examined more closely, evaluated more deeply, and remembered more clearly than information with positive or neutral implications (e.g., Baumeister et al., 2001). This "negativity bias" is also prominent in contemporary political behavior research (e.g., Lau, 1982; Soroka et al., 2019). Compelling evidence of the attractive power of negative information is provided in a pair of experimental studies reported in Soroka (2014). Using psychophysiological indicators of attentiveness (measures of heart rate and skin conductance levels), Soroka studied responses to televised news content and political advertising, finding higher levels of activation and attentiveness when research participants were exposed to negative stories/ads than when they were exposed to positive content (Soroka, 2014, pp. 101–106).

Scholars of retrospective voting have made prominent contributions to political behavior research concerning negativity bias. Indeed, likely the earliest evidence of negativity bias in the subfield concerns the possible asymmetry of punishment and reward in economic voting (Bloom and Price, 1975; but see Park, 2019). However, experimental work on negativity bias in retrospective voting is, to our knowledge, nonexistent.

In principle, Experiments 1 and 2 can provide post hoc tests of negativity bias. To the extent that our participants' performance appraisals are informed by the distribution of worker types, we might assume that the distribution's average (1,200 units) defines the neutral reference point in relation to which performance is appraised as positive (above average) or negative (below average). We can then test for asymmetry in the impact of negative and positive deviations from this implied neutral point. If we do so, we find only suggestive evidence of negativity bias in performance evaluation.[27]

---

[27] To construct this test, we pool data from Experiments 1 and 2. We define variables that capture exposure to positive and negative performance information, such that positive (negative)

However, we regard this as a weak test of negativity bias as we are doubtful many participants' appraisals are directly shaped by the 1,200-unit average of worker types. As we observed in Experiment 1, distinctions in worker retention are much sharper at the extremes of observed worker performance, which is consistent with different participants' applying a range of different (albeit interrelated) appraisal strategies. These strategies, in turn, may vary significantly in the neutral points they imply, and these neutral points may not be well summarized by the average of worker types.

To provide a stronger test of negativity bias, we adapt the baseline game such that it provides a single, clear reference point in relation to which participants can appraise performance as positive or negative. More specifically, we present Worker A's weekly output as a deviation from the average rather than presenting absolute performance. For instance, if a worker produces 1,300 units one week, we inform participants that the worker has produced "100 units above the historical average." In this way, we can more confidently make assumptions regarding the valence of participants' appraisals and, as such, provide a more convincing test of negativity bias in performance evaluation.

We also seek to increase our power to detect asymmetries by eliminating extraneous variance in performance. Rather than select worker types at random from the uniform distribution, we assign Experiment 3 participants to one of three incumbent profiles: either a "neutral," "positive," or "negative" performance condition. Each profile consists of a fixed set of weekly performances. For the positive condition, we draw 16 weekly outputs from a normal distribution with a mean of 1,350 and express each as a deviation from the factory average ($W_{pos} \sim N(1350 - 1200, 250)$). The "negative" profile is simply the positive deviations with the opposite valence ($W_{neg} = -1 * W_{pos}$). Finally, the performance values in the neutral profile are equal to those in the negative condition plus 150 ($W_{neutral} = W_{neg} + 150$). The realized means of worker performance, expressed as deviations from the mean of worker types, are -149.2 (negative condition), 0.8 (neutral condition), and 149.2 (positive condition).[28] These changes eliminate two sources of random variation across participants, with a view to reducing the overall variability of retention.

---

performance is the average of positive (negative) deviations from 1,200. We then regress worker retention on the performance information variables, ignoring Experiment 2's variance manipulation, which had no significant effects. Coefficient estimates on both variables are positive and statistically significant (at the 99 percent level) and, on its face, the coefficient on negative performance is 75 percent larger than that on positive performance. However, the difference between coefficients is not significant ($p = 0.14$).

[28] Note also that the mean of worker performance in the neutral condition deviates slightly from the "true" reference point (zero), which allows us to express performance using only integers.

The logic of the design is to observe and compare retention when perform-ance is equal to the reference point – i.e., the mean of worker types – and when it is a fixed number of units above or below it. If participants respond to perform-ance asymmetrically – punishing poor performance more harshly than good performance is rewarded – then we would expect the absolute difference in the probability of retention to be larger between the negative and neutral conditions than between the positive and neutral conditions.[29]

4.3.2 Results

A total of 689 participants completed Experiment 3. Figure 5(A) displays the three treatment profiles for reference and Figure 5(B) shows the "deviation" output screen.[30] Figure 5(C) reports a regression of incumbent retention on indicators for assignment to the positive and negative performance profiles (relative to assignment to the neutral profile). The coefficients on these indica-tors are sensibly positive and negative, respectively, consistent with the assump-tion that the "historical average" defines an intuitive reference point for the appraisal of worker performance. Figure 5(D) presents an interesting compari-son: The roughly 60-point retention difference between the positive and nega-tive conditions suggests a somewhat larger performance vote than in either Experiment 1 or 2. Whereas Experiments 1 and 2 imply an increase of between 7 and 11 points in the probability of retention as production increases by 100

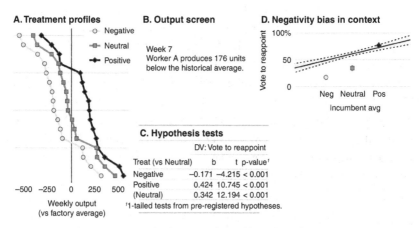

Figure 5 Exploring negativity bias, Experiment 3

---

[29] This expectation is registered here: https://doi.org/10.17605/OSF.IO/5E4GT.

[30] To clarify the presentation, within profiles, the weekly performance values are ordered from lowest to highest. As described in the main text, the order in which values are reported to participants is randomized across participants.

units, the comparison of Experiment 3's negative and positive conditions implies (assuming linearity) an increase of roughly 20 points in the retention probability for every 100 units of increased production. The difference likely reflects the salience of the historical average in the appraisal process: Relative to Experiments 1 and 2, a larger share of participants in Experiment 3 are likely to directly incorporate the factory average in their appraisal strategy. This comparison reveals the power of suggesting explicit performance appraisals – short-circuiting the integration-appraisal processes – as most prior experimental designs do.

While the effect of performance is sizable, we see no evidence of the anticipated negativity bias. In fact, what we observe is a seeming *positivity* bias, with the retention difference between the positive and neutral conditions nearly three times that of the neutral-negative difference ($p < 0.001$). These results are strikingly inconsistent with a well-established empirical regularity (though perhaps not so well-established as regards retrospective voting: see Park, 2019) and suggest that negativity bias may be limited, or even nonexistent, in this domain.

That said, we note an alternative interpretation that is consistent with negativity bias and, furthermore, suggests an important insight regarding the relationship between integration and appraisal. Recall from Section 1 that we are agnostic about the sequence in which integration and appraisal of performance information might occur, allowing that integration may follow appraisal, in whole or in part, and vice versa. However, theories of negativity bias can yield different predictions regarding performance evaluation depending on whether appraisal comes before or after integration. If we conceptualize negativity bias as the assignment of greater evaluative weight to negative than positive appraisals of performance, it matters significantly whether those weights are applied before or after the information is integrated.

Our implicit premise for Experiment 3 was that integration precedes appraisal: that participants would, first, integrate an impression of performance based on the average of weekly performance and, second, form an appraisal based on that impression. Given this integration-then-appraisal assumption, our logic requires that the negative and positive conditions are equally dissimilar (in absolute terms) from the neutral condition: Average performance in the neutral condition (~ 0 units/week) is roughly 149 units below that in the positive condition and 149 units above that in the negative condition. Under an appraisal-then-integration logic, however, unequal weighting of negative and positive weekly performances implies that, in the neutral condition, above- and below-average weekly performances will *not* cancel out in the process of being averaged into an overall impression. Consequently, average performance in the neutral condition would be deflected below zero – and a crucial assumption of our design (i.e., that the negative and positive conditions are equally dissimilar, in performance terms, from the neutral condition) would be violated.

While this combination of negativity bias and the assumption that integration follows appraisal in the performance evaluation process can explain Experiment 3's results, we emphasize the post hoc nature of this argument. At the same time, the results are clearly inconsistent with a model premised on symmetrical weighting of positive and negative performance information: Under such a model, retention rates in the negative and positive conditions should be roughly equidistant from the neutral condition, whether integration precedes or follows appraisal.

4.4 Experiment 4: Does Timing Matter?

4.4.1 Design and Expectations

Economic voting scholars have long suspected that voters place more emphasis on recent than long-term change in economic conditions (e.g., Kiewiet and Rivers, 1984). Emblematic of this assumption are standard survey measures of retrospective economic evaluations, which generally ask how conditions have changed over the preceding year. Observational studies of such "recency bias" in the economic vote, typically relying on analysis of aggregate economic and political data, generally conclude that the assumption behind the survey measures tracks voters' behavior reasonably well (Achen and Bartels, 2016).

Healy and Lenz (2014), in an extensive experimental investigation, connect the findings on the economy to a broader psychological literature on "retrospective assessment" in a variety of domains. They also usefully identify possible explanations for recency bias in political contexts, arguing that it may reflect poor memory for earlier experiences, a belief that recent experiences are more informative regarding future outcomes, or (as they conclude) a manifestation of "attribute substitution," that is, relying on a readily available "related attribute" instead of a more-difficult-to-obtain "target attribute" (p. 33). Notably, in addition to adducing considerable evidence of recency bias in economic evaluation, Healy and Lenz identify the same pattern in the area of crime performance (p. 16). Pereira and Waterbury (2019) generalize recency bias to government integrity, finding that the negative electoral consequences of scandal outbreaks for members of the US House of Representatives fade quickly.

Alternatively, rather than the most recent information carrying outsize weight in performance evaluations, voters may be disproportionately affected by the first information they encounter in a stream of performance, a dynamic we label "primacy bias." Stiers et al. (2020) suggest that, if voters process performance information "online" – updating their overall impression of performance continuously as new information is encountered – then early information may be "of particular importance" (p. 649). As Lodge, McGraw, and Stroh (1989) explain, online models of information processing imply that "impressions formed early in the process guide both the subsequent encoding and retrieval of information, as well as evaluations" (pp. 414–415). In the context of performance evaluation, the implication is that appraisals formed on the basis of initial performance may shape appraisals of later performance, pulling the latter in the direction of the former.

As in the case of negativity bias, we can use data from Experiments 1 and 2 to evaluate arguments regarding recency and primacy bias. We modeled incumbent retention across the pooled sample as a function of average performance from week 1 to 12 and average performance from week 13 to 16. While the coefficient on late performance is, on its face, roughly 75 percent the size of that on early performance,[31] the relevant test is the *ratio* of these coefficients. Given that the early average reflects three times the information of the late average, unbiased integration of performance information implies that the late average should be no greater than one-third the size of its early counterpart. The probability of the null for this hypothesis – i.e., that the ratio of the early to the late coefficient differs from 3:1 – is 0.367. In fact, the ratio of these coefficients is approximately 1.4:1, implying that recent performance counts for more than early performance.

We build on this result with the design of Experiment 4, which aims to increase our power to detect recency and primacy effects. The basic logic is to adapt the baseline game such that we hold constant the worker's performance profile, while varying only the order in which weekly performance values are realized. That is, every participant observes exactly the same set of outputs, but we manipulate the order of their presentation. By holding the mean and variance of performance constant, we eliminate two important potential determinants of retention and, thus, reduce the overall variability of the outcome. To identify recency and primacy effects, we vary whether a "spell" consisting of the four worst weeks of performance comes early (in weeks 1–4) or late (in weeks 13–16) and compare retention in these conditions with a control in which the four worst weeks occur randomly throughout the sixteen weeks. In the early and late conditions, the order of the spell of bad weeks is randomized across participants, as is the order of the "non-spell" weeks.[32]

---

[31] This difference is not significant at conventional levels.

[32] Another change from the baseline design is that we omit from the instructions the stipulation that the "pattern of production typically does not change over time" to allow for the manifestation of recency bias that reflects the belief that later outcomes are more informative than earlier ones.

If recency bias prevails in the processing of performance information, then worker retention should be lower in the late condition than in the control, given that the worker's worst weeks will weigh more heavily if they all occur at the end than if they are evenly spread across the worker's tenure in the factory. Conversely, primacy bias implies that retention should be lower in the early condition than in the control. These are not conflicting expectations, of course; we may find evidence that both initial and recent performance weigh disproportionately in retention decisions.[33]

4.4.2 Results

Seven hundred and sixty-four participants completed Experiment 4. Figure 6(A) highlights the different performance profiles, with the drop in incumbent performance coming early, late, or randomly. Figure 6(B)–(C) presents retention rates by assignment to treatment condition. The results provide striking evidence of recency bias. Keeping in mind that all participants observe exactly the same sixteen weeks of performance, the difference between the late condition and the control indicates a 14-point reduction in the probability of retention when a worker's worst weeks happen to fall at the end of, rather than randomly throughout, their tenure in the factory ($p = 0.001$). This effect is equal

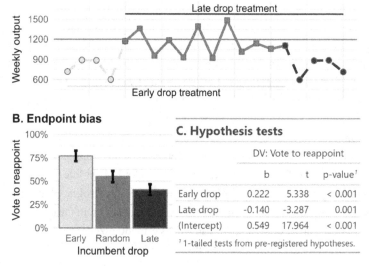

Figure 6 Overweighting recent performance, Experiment 4

---

[33] These expectations are registered here: https://doi.org/10.17605/OSF.IO/SQ426.

to the impact of reducing a worker's weekly production by 127 (Experiment 1) or possibly as many as 200 units (Experiment 2).

Conversely, we find no evidence of primacy bias. On the contrary, the probability of retention in the early condition is fully 22 points *higher* than in the control ($p < 0.001$). While we did not preregister this reasoning, we note that the result is also consistent with recency bias. That is, given that the worst weeks in the early condition necessarily do *not* fall at the end, average performance in the final weeks of this condition should be relatively better than in the control.

One possible objection to our design is that whether or not poor performance occurs in four-week spells is confounded with assignment to the early and late conditions. This would be problematic if, for example, grouping similar performances together increases their salience. Be that as it may, salience alone cannot account for the pattern we observe, given that, far from being lower, retention is in fact much higher in the early condition than in the control.

4.5 Summary

In this section, we present original tests of retrospective voting theory that allow individuals to integrate and appraise performance autonomously. To a degree that is unique in the literature, we do not short-circuit this central challenge of retrospective voting. We establish, in Experiment 1, that citizens can indeed make reasonable sense of a variable stream of performance information, integrating and appraising their own impressions of worker performance. This experiment also suggests a possible bias in favor of incumbents, as perfectly average workers are retained at a rate above that implied by a risk-neutral strategy. Experiment 2 tests for responsiveness to the variability of incumbent performance. Here, we see no evidence that participants were drawn to more stable performers or that higher-variance signals frustrated their capacity to identify competence. Experiment 3 tests for the presence of negativity bias and also yields a null finding. That said, our analysis highlights a critical point: If we study retrospective voting in a way that allows the integration-appraisal task to unfold "naturally," then it may sometimes be necessary to theorize the task explicitly, particularly the sequencing of integration and appraisal. In the case of Experiment 3, whether the results are consistent with negativity bias depends on whether one assumes that integration precedes appraisal (as we did) or vice versa. Finally, in Experiment 4, we find striking evidence of recency bias and no evidence at all of primacy bias. Simply shifting the order of otherwise equivalent performance profiles has a large effect on retention of incumbent workers.

5 Retrospective Voting under Interdependence

In Section 4, we presented tests of retrospective voting theory that, unlike nearly all past experimental research in this area, challenged participants to integrate and appraise performance information. The designs of these experiments are faithful to the core elements of retrospective voting theory, as exemplified in classic accounts (e.g., Downs, 1957; Key, 1966; Fiorina, 1981). Yet they neglect an important complication highlighted by contemporary scholars: the problem of interdependent performance.

We have emphasized the streaming nature of performance information. However, the only source of variation we have considered to this point is random noise. Voters in an age of globalization face a much steeper challenge in that the changes they observe in well-being also reflect an additional source of variation: spillover from actors and events beyond the incumbent's control. Put simply, as performance *here* is increasingly tied to performance *over there*, it becomes more challenging for citizens to identify the unique contribution of the only political actors they are in a position to punish and reward: the incumbent officeholders appearing on their ballots on Election Day.

Evaluating government performance in the context of interdependence – integrating and appraising over multiple, confounded streams of information – is a fundamental challenge of representative democracy. Past research has focused on how voters judge governments' economic performances under globalization (Duch and Stevenson, 2008; Kayser and Peress, 2012), though the generic problem of interdependent performance outcomes confounds voting over a wide range of issues and across levels of government. Success in reducing a city's gun violence, for instance, depends in part on gun control and law enforcement efforts in other jurisdictions (e.g., Pierce et al., 2004). Voters in all such contexts confront the challenge of integrating and appraising information regarding performance outcomes that are driven by the efforts of numerous actors. The failure to integrate and appraise this information in a way that allows voters to judge incumbents for "their" part in the process disrupts the accountability function of elections. In the worst-case scenario, an above-average incumbent fails to be reelected owing to spillover from below-average performance in other jurisdictions.

Note an important distinction here between interdependent and collectively produced outcomes. While both are multiagent processes in which the agents' individual efforts are unknown to the principal, agents in collectives work toward a joint outcome (e.g., the parties of a governing coalition fighting unemployment). Moreover, voters evaluating collectively produced outcomes typically have the power to discipline every member of the collective. The challenge is identifying each agent's power within the group (see, e.g., Powell, 2000). By contrast, interdependence is the contingency of performance on the efforts of multiple agents, including agents beyond the voter's electoral reach. The challenge is unmasking the performance of the agents the voter can discipline, independent of the spillover from external actors.

How do voters judge incumbent quality when performance is interdependent? In this section, we investigate this question in a series of experiments that modify the baseline game such that the performance of the incumbent worker is obscured by that of one or more "comparators" – other workers in the factory. We begin, in Section 5.1, by presenting three competing theories regarding how performance-oriented voters manage the integration-appraisal task where performance outcomes are interdependent.

5.1 Three Theories of Retrospective Voting under Interdependence

Prior research suggests three ways in which integration and appraisal unfold in the context of interdependence: blind retrospection, rational discounting, and benchmark processing. The most concerning perspective for advocates of representative democracy is *blind retrospection* (Achen and Bartels, 2016). In this view, voters never consciously confront the problem of extra-local spillover. Instead, integration and appraisal are indiscriminate, and voters reward and punish incumbents for aggregate results, including those beyond their control. Prior studies find, for example, that voters take authorities to task for droughts (e.g., Cole et al., 2012), sporting outcomes (e.g., Healy and Malhotra, 2010), shark attacks (Achen and Bartels, 2016), and, in the critical domain of economic performance, market shocks from other countries (e.g., Leigh and McLeish, 2009; Hayes et al., 2015; Campello and Zucco, 2016) and other levels of government (e.g., Gelineau and Remmer, 2006). Moreover, performance judgments are seen to be myopic (e.g., Healy and Lenz, 2014) and biased by exogenous shocks (e.g., Huber et al., 2012; but see Fowler and Montagnes, 2015).

In sharp contrast, *rational discounting* suggests that citizens recognize the extent to which interdependence limits a government's "room to maneuver" and that the integration-appraisal process reflects this (e.g., Hellwig, 2001, 2008). Duch and Stevenson (2008; see also Alesina and Rosenthal, 1995) argue that voters isolate the government's contribution to economic performance by discounting economic movement[34] in proportion to the ratio of the variance

---

[34] That is, unexpected variance that does not reflect the natural rate of economic growth or prior decisions of electorally dependent actors (Duch and Stevenson, 2008, p. 141).

of competence shocks, which reflect the government's efforts, to the variance of exogenous shocks, which reflect spillover from other jurisdictions. Interdependence amplifies the noise from spillover and inhibits voters from seeing the government's efforts underneath changes in well-being. In response, voters learn to discount for broader trends, attributing a larger share of performance to external forces.

Prior observational studies show that voters behave "as if" they integrate and appraise performance data as rational discounting theory predicts. Voters appear to be aware of unexpected macroeconomic shocks (e.g., Duch and Stevenson, 2010) and, in open economies, are less likely to report that elected officials hold sway over economic outcomes (e.g., Alcañiz and Hellwig, 2011). Voters also appear less likely to reward or punish incumbents for national economic conditions in open economies (e.g., Duch and Stevenson, 2008). Furthermore, citizens discriminate between local and national performance (Ebeid and Rodden, 2006), and judgments of responsibility adapt when policymaking authority passes to lower levels of government (León, 2012; Larsen, 2019).

The final alternative is *benchmarking*.[35] Benchmarking voters assess government competence by comparing local outcomes to a referent or peer group. If states in an interdependent network experience the same shocks, then local deviations from the common trend become the key marker of government stewardship. What matters is not performance per se; rather, benchmarking voters reward incumbents who outperform their peers and punish those who underperform.

The benchmarking thesis follows from research on evaluative judgment in social psychology and public administration. Social comparison theory (Festinger, 1954) suggests that citizens gauge performance – their own and others' – in relation to a referent or comparator. These relative assessments are especially likely in complex informational environments like the ones voters face in an open, interdependent economy (Kayser and Peress, 2012). Experimental research suggests that benchmark processing is innate (e.g., Mussweiler, 2003) and automatic (e.g., Gilbert et al., 1995); that confidence in a benchmark comparison rises with the availability of a suitable referent (e.g., Gastorf and Suls, 1978); and that individuals are more responsive to social (external/spatial) referents than to historical (internal/temporal) ones (e.g., Charbonneau and Van Ryzin, 2015). Olsen (2017) shows that relative retrospective voting is weaker where lines of authority for performance outcomes are blurred by the inputs of other actors.

---

[35] Benchmarking is sometimes referred to as "relative performance voting" (e.g., Aytaç, 2018) or, in economics, a "yardstick" response (e.g., Holmstrom, 1982; Besley and Case, 1995).

Consistent with the benchmarking perspective, prior studies suggest that voters around the world evaluate national economic well-being relative to cross-national and international averages (e.g., Kayser and Peress, 2012; Hansen et al., 2015; Aytaç, 2018) and, in the United States, judge state economic performance against national outcomes (Cohen, 2020). Moreover, voters seem to rely on similar or connected peer countries as referents (Park, 2019). Importantly, benchmarking in these studies can be understood as a means of extracting an estimate of the incumbent's contribution to local performance or as a strategy for appraising local performance. If, for instance, the economy of a state in a wheat-exporting region is growing at an annual rate of 4 percent, while neighboring states are growing at an average rate of 6 percent, the voter may see the difference – a 2-point *contraction* – as the incumbent government's contribution to growth. In this way, the benchmark (the average of neighboring states) is used to extract an estimate of the endogenous component of local performance (the incumbent's contribution).[36]

These rival accounts of retrospective voting under interdependence – blind retrospection, rational discounting, and benchmarking – paint clear but distinct pictures of the mechanisms guiding the integration and appraisal process. Paradoxically, existing literature supplies evidence consistent with each approach, though largely in observational studies. The relevant experimental literature, as we note in Section 1, typically short-circuits one or both steps of the integration-appraisal process. We are left, then, with few diagnostic tests of the mechanisms that drive the retrospective voting relationship. The experimental designs we employ in the remainder of this section help fill this gap.

5.2 Experiment 5: Can Voters Unmask Incumbent Competence?

5.2.1 Design

The baseline game excludes the problem of interdependent outcomes: The incumbent worker's output reflects their underlying type, plus random variation. To study retrospective voting under interdependence, we must introduce a stream of exogenous variation that is systematic and, critically, *knowable*. If the exogenous variation were not knowable – in the sense that it is possible to

---

[36] Conversely, a voter in this scenario may be unaware of the problem of interdependent outcomes yet still evaluate their incumbent's economic performance relative to that of neighboring states, using the benchmark (6 percent growth) to form a negative appraisal of local performance. These two interpretations have equivalent implications in observational studies of the impact of relative performance, provided we assume that extraction-oriented voters form neutral appraisals of zero growth.

acquire information about its parameters – then the modification of the baseline game would be trivial: that is, the exogenous variation would be just another source of random variation in performance. More importantly, the knowability of exogenous sources of performance variation is required to study models of retrospective voting under interdependence, given that they assume voters have access to information regarding peer jurisdictions (Duch and Stevenson, 2008; Kayser and Peress, 2012).

We develop two designs in this section that incorporate exogenous variation in performance through the introduction of a "comparator" worker, a peer who operates alongside the incumbent and whose performance obscures the incumbent's contributions to total factory production. These "multi-stream" games – which present more than one stream of performance information – begin with the comparator working alone in the factory for eight weeks. We then introduce the incumbent's output to the same stream for the next eight weeks. How incumbent performance enters the stream differs between the "unmasking" and "recognition" designs. Table 2 presents the flow of these games (Row A) and the composition of factory output before and after the incumbent's arrival (Row B).

Experiment 5 relies on the unmasking game design. The game instructions advise participants that the incumbent's arrival is delayed for reasons beyond their control, and the game begins with the comparator working alone, with total factory performance equal only to the comparator's production ($F_{pre} = C_{pre}$). Participants, then, have eight weeks to learn about the comparator's performance (i.e., the exogenous variation), should they wish to apply this information to their retention decisions. The incumbent arrives in week 9, at which point

Table 2 Designs for retrospective voting under interdependence

A. Flow of multi-stream games

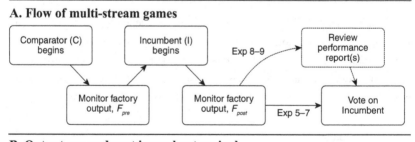

B. Output pre and post incumbent arrival

Game design	Output, F_{pre}	Incumbent begins	Output, F_{post}
Unmasking	C_{pre}	I works alongside C	$C_{post} + I_{post}$
Recognition	C_{pre}	C quits; I replaces	I_{post}

factory output reflects the combined efforts of both workers ($F_{post} = C_{post} + I_{post}$). Indeed, participants in the unmasking game *never* observe the incumbent's performance directly. In this way, the design challenges participants to use their knowledge of the comparator[37] to extract information about incumbent performance. After week 16, participants must decide whether to reappoint or replace their incumbent; no decision is made regarding the comparator, who continues in the factory irrespective of the incumbent's fate.[38]

A key feature of the Experiment 5 unmasking game is that we manipulate the variance of the comparator's output. Specifically, we randomly assign participants to either a high-variance ($C_t \sim N(\mu_C, 250)$) or low-variance $C_t \sim N(\mu_C, 100)$ comparator.[39] As explained in Section 5.2.3, this permits a clear test of the rational discounting mechanism, allowing us to see if the response to factory performance weakens with the variance of spillover.

The information regarding worker characteristics in Experiment 5 does not substantively differ from that in the baseline experiment.[40] When the incumbent starts in the factory, we emphasize this feature of the design, noting that "the factory total now equals the units produced by [the incumbent] plus the units produced by [the comparator]." To underline the exogenous nature of the comparator's performance, the instructions stipulate that the workers "work independently" and "operate different machines" and that "the performance of one worker is unrelated to the performance of the other." That said, while the exogenous variation in this design is logically irrelevant to the evaluation in question, it reflects performance both in the same domain and by a highly similar actor. In this way, we analogize the confounding of the behavior of multiple governments in producing performance outcomes.[41]

---

[37] Note that we never present a summary of comparator performance to participants in the multi-stream games, although participants can choose to acquire such information in Experiment 8 (see Section 6.1).

[38] Strictly speaking, the sequential presentation of workers, such that information about the comparator always appears first, creates temporal variation between the workers. In practice, however, participants acquire information about the workers nearly simultaneously, completing the entire experiment in about six minutes, on average.

[39] We selected values of the noise parameters such that the task of extracting performance is neither trivially easy (low-noise condition) nor unreasonably difficult (high-noise condition) and so that, in expectation, we would avoid a sizable number of negative values of revealed performance.

[40] One stylistic change from the baseline experiment is that the instructions indicate the workers completed "a training course to prepare them to work in the factory," whereas the baseline design simply notes the worker is "fully trained to work in any department."

[41] This feature of the design is an important contrast with Huber et al.'s (2012) study of voter responsiveness to "irrelevant information." In their design, the irrelevant information is

5.2.2 Expectations

A primary advantage of our experimental approach is that we independently manipulate the underlying components of performance – i.e., exogenous variation and the endogenous contribution of the incumbent. This allows us to define clear tests of each theory of retrospective voting in terms of how individuals process information about incumbent performance relative to spillover.

To analyze the results of Experiment 5, we model the decision to retain the incumbent as a function of average factory production before and after the incumbent's arrival, $F_{pre,i}$ and $F_{post,i}$:

$$Reappoint_i = \alpha F_{pre,i} + \beta F_{post,i} + \theta + u_i, \tag{1}$$

where $Reappoint_i$ is a binary indicator of i's vote to extend the incumbent's contract; α and β are the weights attached to factory performance at each stage; θ is the intercept; and u_i is an error term. Note that factory production captures the sum of incumbent and comparator output (i.e., $F_{pre,i} = I_{pre,i} + C_{pre,i}$). However, the incumbent's late arrival means that $I_{pre,i} = 0$, and factory production reduces to the comparator's average ($F_{pre,i} = C_{pre,i}$).

Table 3 summarizes the behavior implied by each theoretical model in terms of the expected values of α and β. Blind retrospection describes a voter who does not distinguish between local and extra-local sources of performance. At a minimum, this voter rewards incumbents for combined factory output during the incumbent's tenure ($\beta > 0$). Whether they respond to prior performance,

Table 3 Implied response to factory performance by approach

Retrospective voting theory	Parameters (see Eq. 1)	
	Pre-incumbent tenure, $F_{pre,i}$	Incumbent's tenure, $F_{post,i}$
Blind retrospection	$\alpha = 0$	$\beta > 0$
Blind retrospection, indiscriminate	$\alpha > 0$	$\beta > 0$
Rational discounting	$\alpha = 0$	$\beta > 0, \beta = f(\kappa)$
Benchmark comparison	$\alpha < 0$	$\beta > 0$

presented as a surprise on a separate screen and in a distinct format, and it arises from a distinct process, a "lottery." In effect, Huber and colleagues' participants are challenged to *ignore* the lottery outcome, whereas participants in Experiment 5 must *attend* to the irrelevant information (i.e., the comparator's production) to extract information about the evaluative target's performance.

$F_{pre,i}$, is unclear. If we assume that subjects recognize the start of the incumbent's tenure, then they ought to ignore comparator performance prior to the incumbent's arrival ($\alpha = 0$) but fail to account for the weight of the comparator's efforts during the incumbent's tenure. A more extreme reading of the theory might suggest that evaluation in our game is completely indiscriminate – that is, subjects fail to recognize the start of the incumbent's tenure. In this case, the blindly retrospective voter may reward the incumbent for factory performance prior to their arrival ($\alpha > 0$). We note both versions in Table 3.

In contrast, the rational discounter parses observed factory output to credit the incumbent for some portion thereof. In Duch and Stevenson's (2008) influential formulation, voters discount their response to performance by a "competency signal" equal to the ratio of the variance of the incumbent's contribution to the variance of total output. Applying their formalization to our design, the response to factory performance, β, is conditioned by a competency signal, κ_i, such that $\beta = f(\kappa_i)$, where $f(\cdot)$ is a positive function. This signal reflects the incumbent's relative contribution to the variance of factory production in weeks 9 to 16:

$$\kappa_i = \frac{Var(I_{post,i})}{Var(F_{post,i})}, \tag{2}$$

where $Var(I_{post,i})$ and $Var(F_{post,i})$ are the respective variances of the incumbent's production and total factory production in weeks 9 to 16 ($0 \leq \kappa \leq 1$). Substantively, higher values of κ_i indicate that factory output provides more information about incumbent competence, and participants credit (blame) incumbents for a larger share of the yield.

In Experiment 5, subjects can estimate the competency signal based on the difference in output variance before and after the incumbent's arrival.[42] The discounting voter is unmoved by the comparator's efforts prior to the incumbent's arrival ($\alpha = 0$) and rewards incumbent performance ($\beta > 0$). Further, and critically, the model implies that the sensitivity of the reappointment decision to factory output rises with the clarity of the competency signal: e.g., $\beta_{\kappa=.8} > \beta_{\kappa=.2}$.[43]

---

[42] Specifically, the discounting thesis implies that participants will estimate the signal as:

$$\hat{\kappa}_i = \frac{Var(F_{post,i}) - Var(C_{pre,i})}{Var(F_{post,i})}.$$

We substitute $Var(F_{post,i}) - Var(C_{pre,i})$ for $Var(I_{post,i})$, given $Var(C_{pre,i}) = Var(C_{post,i})$.

[43] Note that our approach allows that subjects may be less-than-perfect discounters: we assume only that β is some positive function of κ.

Finally, benchmark processors identify the incumbent's competence in the difference between local performance and an extra-local referent. In our game, this implies, first, that the probability of reappointing the incumbent rises with factory output during the incumbent's tenure, even though it may reflect a combination of local and extra-local forces ($\beta > 0$). Second, and most importantly, the model implies that reappointment becomes less likely with prior production, i.e., in the presence of a competent, though otherwise irrelevant, comparator ($\alpha < 0$).[44]

In summary, each model predicts that participants will reward the incumbent for total factory production during their tenure. The role of "spillover" in the voting calculus, however, differs markedly. Rational discounters rely on the comparator's variance to extract a competency signal but are unmoved by the comparator's competence as such. Blindly retrospective voters will, if anything, treat extra-local performance as equivalent to local performance. Benchmarking voters will punish an incumbent for the efforts of a superior comparator.

5.2.3 Results

In the "full sample" column of Table 4, we present estimates of Equation 1, pooling across the two levels of the variance factor. Consistent with all three accounts of retrospective voting under interdependence, we observe a systematic response to factory output during the incumbent worker's tenure. Specifically, a 100-unit increase in average production increases the probability of reappointment by 0.135 ($Pr(\beta \leq 0) < 0.001$).

The critical estimate for discriminating among the theories, however, is $\hat{\alpha}$. And the result is clear: The probability of retaining the incumbent declines by 0.093 as factory production prior to the incumbent's arrival increases by 100 units. This result is consistent with the benchmarking hypothesis ($Pr(\alpha \geq 0) < 0.001$) and contrary to both blind retrospection (which implies ignoring or rewarding the incumbent for the comparator's performance) and rational discounting (which implies no response).[45]

The next two columns of Table 4 break down the pattern of response by levels of the variance factor. As defined in Equation 2, participants in the low-variance condition received a strong competency signal ($\kappa = 250^2/(250^2 + 100^2) = 0.86$), whereas those in the high-variance condition received a weak competency signal ($\kappa = 250^2/(250^2 + 250^2) = 0.5$). To

---

[44] Some might prefer that we estimate the response to the performance gap directly, substituting $F_{post,i} - F_{pre,i}$ into Equation 1, but these specifications are equivalent (Arel-Bundock et al., 2019).

[45] Given rational discounting, we would observe a negative $\hat{\alpha}$ when estimating Equation 1 in the presence of a positive correlation between comparator performance and the variance of comparator performance. However, these quantities are uncorrelated by design in our experiments.

Table 4 Unmasking incumbent performance, Experiment 5

		Retrospective voting by treatment arm		
	Full sample	Low-variance comparator $\kappa = 0.86$	High-variance comparator $\kappa = 0.50$	Difference
Output, pre-incumbent (α)	−0.093	−0.125	−0.071	
	(0.010)	(0.016)	(0.013)	
High-variance effect, Δ_α				*0.054*
$Pr(\Delta_\alpha \leq 0)$				*0.005*
Output, incumbent's tenure (β)	0.135	0.164	0.117	
	(0.014)	(0.021)	(0.018)	
High-variance effect, Δ_β				*−0.048*
$Pr(\Delta_\beta \geq 0)$				*0.045*
Intercept (θ)	0.251	0.278	0.223	
	(0.145)	(0.210)	(0.201)	
Hypothesis tests by treatment				
No retrospective voting, $Pr(\beta \leq 0)$	< 0.001	< 0.001	< 0.001	
No benchmark comparison, $Pr(\alpha \geq 0)$	< 0.001	< 0.001	< 0.001	

Note. Ordinary least squares (OLS) estimates of the choice to reappoint the incumbent. Standard errors in parentheses. Output scaled in 100s of units. N = 849.

be sure, we have already ruled out a pure version of the rational discounting theory, given the negative impact of factory output prior to the incumbent's arrival. Nonetheless, even assuming the benchmarking logic, the higher variance of the comparator's output in the weak signal condition may render inferences about both components of the benchmarker's evaluation ($F_{pre,i}$ and $F_{post,i}$) more uncertain. This uncertainty, in turn, may reduce the impact of these components on the probability of incumbent retention. This expectation is consistent with our reasoning, in Section 4.2, regarding the impact of variability on evaluation of incumbents.

And indeed, the results accord with this argument. Subjects in both the weak and strong signal treatment conditions followed the same pattern of benchmark evaluation as the full sample. However, those assigned to a high-variance comparator ($\kappa = 0.50$) were less responsive both to factory production during the incumbent's tenure ($\beta_{\kappa=0.86} - \beta_{\kappa=0.50} = -0.048$) *and* to production prior to the incumbent's arrival in the factory ($\alpha_{\kappa=0.86} - \alpha_{\kappa=0.50} = 0.054$). Both differences are statistically significant. While these results are somewhat surprising, considering the null findings regarding variability in Section 4, the difference may simply reflect the relative complexity of the evaluative tasks in question – that is, the fact that participants in Experiment 5, unlike those in Experiment 2, must confront multiple streams of performance information.

In summary, the results of Experiment 5 point toward benchmarking as the default mode of evaluation for our participants.[46] We also find, sensibly, that higher-variance performance streams inhibit responsiveness, again via the benchmarking mechanism (cf. Olsen, 2017).

5.3 Experiment 6: Can Voters Recognize Incumbent Competence?

While the results of Experiment 5 favor the benchmarking theory over the alternatives, one possible criticism is that the unmasking game unduly tilts the scales toward comparative evaluation. For one thing, the initial part of the task (i.e., weeks 1–8) strongly focuses attention on comparator performance. For another, the incumbent's arrival in the factory is announced along with a reminder that the stream of performance information – "the factory total" – is the sum of comparator and incumbent production. These two features of the design may invite participants to treat comparator performance as a benchmark in evaluating factory performance in the second part of the task (i.e., weeks 9–16).

The "recognition" design of Experiment 6 (outlined in Table 2) aims to address this criticism. Here, the instructions advise that participants are required to evaluate

---

[46] That said, we do not observe "full benchmarking" (i.e., $(-\alpha) \neq \beta$). Whether this is the result of imperfect benchmarking or evidence that some participants rely on a different mechanism is unclear.

the performance of a single worker over a sixteen-week period. Indeed, the instructions for Experiment 6 are precisely the same as in the baseline game. However, after week 8, we announce to participants that their worker has "unexpectedly left the factory" and that the worker has already been replaced; we also remind participants of the distribution of worker types. The new worker, now the evaluative target or incumbent, completes the remainder of the sixteen-week evaluation period, after which participants, as always, must choose to reappoint or replace this incumbent.

Critically, the design of Experiment 6 discourages comparative evaluation. While the design does encourage participants to attend to irrelevant information (production in weeks 1–8), in contrast to Experiment 5, there is no signal to unmask. Just as in the Experiment 1 baseline game, participants observe the incumbent in isolation and weekly output, though variable, *is* the uncontaminated competence stream. The task for performance-oriented participants is simply to *recognize* the stream of performance information in weeks 9–16 as a clean indicator of incumbent quality. If, in this context, participants still see the comparator as a baseline for reappointment, it will be strong evidence in support of benchmarking as a default strategy in the integration-appraisal process. Moreover, it will supply direct evidence of the role of benchmarks in performance appraisals, given that, in this setting, the function of benchmarking cannot be to extract the local component of performance.

To analyze the results of Experiment 6, we again estimate Equation 1.[47] The results for 368 participants reveal a systematic benchmarking response. On the one hand, we find that the probability of reappointment increases in direct proportion to the incumbent's average output ($\hat{\beta} = 0.123, Pr(\beta \leq 0) < 0.001$). At the same time, the comparator's early efforts enter the evaluation as a baseline for comparison: Participants punish the incumbent for following a high-performing comparator ($\hat{\alpha} = -0.055$). It is unlikely we observe this response by chance alone ($Pr(\alpha \geq 0) < 0.001$). While the availability of an absolute performance measure is thought to mitigate the drive to compare (Moore and Klein, 2008), these estimates show again that participants identified the incumbent's performance but judged that effort in part for its distinction from a salient comparator.

If the results in Experiment 5 were merely a function of the two features of the unmasking game noted at the start of this section, the benchmarking response should be absent in Experiment 6. Yet the response persists, is large, and is precisely estimated. Together, the results of these two experiments suggest that

---

[47] See Table 6 in Section 7 for complete estimates from Experiments 5–9 and 11.

citizens rely on available benchmarks to judge government performance, even in the presence of absolute measures of competence.

5.4 Experiment 7: How Do Voters Cope with an Incongruent Comparator?

Experiment 7 seeks to address a second possible way in which the designs in this section – both the unmasking design of Experiment 5 and the recognition design of Experiment 6 – may unduly encourage benchmark processing.[48] In particular, a single comparator, as in these designs, may invite a one-to-one comparison that might be less clear or less available in many relevant performance evaluation contexts. After all, in Studies 5 and 6 the comparator's type is drawn from the same uniform distribution as the incumbent's. A less-congruent referent may attenuate or discourage the benchmarking response (Gastorf and Suls, 1978).

Here, we add a second comparator to the unmasking game (see Table 2 for an overview of this design). Instead of observing a single worker's performance in the first eight weeks, participants view the combined output of *two* irrelevant comparators.[49] Upon the incumbent's arrival in week 9, subjects observe eight weeks of total output for all three workers before voting to extend the incumbent's tenure or to hire a replacement. So, rather than a perfectly analogous, apples-to-apples "disturbance," a collective of workers obscures incumbent performance in Experiment 7; in this way, we aim to investigate whether benchmarking emerges in a setting where comparison is less intuitive.

Five hundred and fifty participants completed the experiment. Again, we observe a pattern of benchmark comparison. Ordinary least squares (OLS) estimates of Equation 1[50] show that subjects judged the incumbent for both total factory performance during their tenure ($\hat{\beta} = 0.158$) and the collective-comparator's initial output ($\hat{\alpha} = -0.114$). Both effects are statistically significant, and we reject the null hypothesis of no benchmarking ($Pr(\alpha \geq 0) < 0.001$). Again, the results are also inconsistent with the predictions of blind retrospection and rational discounting models.

---

[48] We registered tests of retrospective voting ($\beta > 0$) and benchmarking ($\alpha < 0$) for this experiment here: https://doi.org/10.17605/OSF.IO/6FNXH. We diverge from the analysis plan with respect to the measurement of the components of performance. Specifically, we follow Arel-Bundock et al. (2019) and model the effect of the observed performance of the comparator and, after the incumbent's arrival, of the comparator and incumbent, rather than the effect of the unobserved, assigned types of the workers. Under the latter specification, the results (reported in the Online Appendix) are substantively similar, although the negative effect of comparator type is not significant.

[49] The joint-comparator's type and weekly output is simply the sum of two comparators: $\mu_{F_{pre,j}} \sim U[1900, 2900]$, $F_{pre} \sim N(\mu_{F_{pre,j}}, 200^2)$.

[50] See Table 6 in Section 7.

5.5 Summary

Confronted with a world in which important outcomes reflect interdependent processes beyond the jurisdiction of any one government, the retrospective voter must adopt a strategy for integration and appraisal that identifies a representative's unique contribution to inherently composite outcomes. Prior observational research suggests that voters are less responsive to performance outcomes where local outcomes are sensitive to extra-local forces. Yet the mechanism underlying this pattern is unclear.

Experiments 5 and 6 revealed a penchant for benchmark processing – an integration-appraisal strategy that relies on external comparison against a peer – even when the comparator's performance is irrelevant. Experiment 7, then, went further in showing that this behavior persists when the referent is incongruous. These findings are notable given the long-standing debate around the psychology of retrospection and the ability of voters in an age of globalization to make sense of their incumbent's contributions to the state of the world. The pattern we observe, of evaluation by comparison to a peer, is also intriguing insofar as our game offers an obvious alternative, "historical" standard of evaluation. Specifically, the game rules indicate – explicitly in some cases – that 1,200 units per week is the historical average for factory workers. Participants appear, then, to bypass this strictly rational benchmark in favor of irrelevant and even incongruous "spatial" referents. Whether this is an indication of how individuals seek out information about incumbent performance is taken up in Section 6.

6 Heuristics and the Problem of Bad Benchmarks

The findings in Section 5 reveal a persistent tendency to apply a strategy of benchmarking to the integration-appraisal process inherent to retrospective voting. The robustness of this tendency across varying contexts suggests that benchmarking may function as a type of cognitive heuristic: an intuitive decision rule or shortcut used to simplify a problem of inference or appraisal. Whereas influential early treatments in political science emphasized the virtues of heuristics as a source of cognitive economy (e.g., Popkin, 1991), later work highlighted the potential pitfalls of reliance on heuristics, particularly among less sophisticated voters who may be less able to use heuristics effectively (Kuklinski and Quirk, 2000; Lau and Redlawsk, 2001). In this regard, a key question concerns voters' capacity to discriminate amongst potential heuristics. Do voters know when it is, and is not, sensible to rely on a given decision rule (Lupia and McCubbins, 1998; Boudreau, 2009)? More specifically, do they know when benchmarking is and is not appropriate?

Section 5's results have mixed implications for this question. In Experiments 5 and 7, benchmarking allows participants to approximately separate incumbent performance from that of irrelevant comparators and, thus, judge the incumbent's contribution to the factory's output. In Experiment 6, however, benchmarking leads participants astray. Benchmarking cannot function as an extraction strategy here as there is nothing to extract; rather, participants are offered an unobstructed look at incumbent competence (i.e., by attending to production after the comparator leaves, and the incumbent arrives, in week 9). It is possible that benchmarking to the comparator constitutes an appraisal strategy in this game, though a suboptimal one: The incumbent is retained at a higher rate as the quality of the comparator declines, notwithstanding that incumbent and comparator performance are unrelated. An optimal appraisal strategy, moreover, is readily available but seemingly not employed by most participants: benchmarking of incumbent performance to the average of worker types.

In this section, we investigate more directly voters' capacity for discrimination in the use of heuristics, focusing on the application of benchmarks to performance evaluation. In Experiment 8, we invite participants to acquire summary information regarding incumbent and comparator performance, allowing us to assess participants' relative "taste" for comparative information. Experiment 9 manipulates the availability of benchmarked and direct indicators of worker performance to examine how the tendency to benchmark varies in the presence of different informational cues. Experiments 10 and 11 zero in on the quality of benchmark use. Experiment 10 documents participants' preferences across benchmarks of varying quality. Finally, Experiment 11 directly considers the sophistication of benchmarking by studying the response to a "shocked" benchmark: a comparator whose performance has been perturbed by outside circumstances beyond their control.

6.1 Experiment 8: Do Voters Want to Benchmark?

Do citizens *want* to benchmark performance? Given the opportunity to acquire incumbent-specific information, will participants nonetheless gravitate toward comparative information? In Experiment 8, we allow participants to uncover summary reports of their workers' performance prior to "voting."

We assigned participants to complete one of the multi-stream games introduced in Section 5, assigning them to the unmasking (i.e., Exp. 5) or recognition (i.e., Exp. 6) design with probabilities 2/3 and 1/3 respectively. The key development is that, immediately prior to voting on the incumbent's reappointment, we invite subjects to select and review *up to two* of the following reports:

(a) Incumbent's average production
(b) Comparator's average production

(c) Difference between the incumbent's and comparator's averages

(d) Total units produced and bonus to date

Only the first report – the incumbent worker's average – contains relevant performance data. In fact, acquiring this report eliminates altogether the need to infer competence from the performance stream. The other reports are irrelevant, though reports (b) and (c) should appeal to benchmark processors.

Our goal in Experiment 8 is to observe information-seeking behavior within the integration-appraisal process. Do individuals *pursue* benchmarked performance data even when absolute metrics of competence are available? If automatic benchmark comparisons can be easily unmade by conscious processes (Gilbert et al., 1995), then participants ought to prefer the direct report of the incumbent's performance. However, if benchmarking is a consciously preferred mode of evaluation, the availability of comparative information should reveal this tendency. Further, the preference for comparative information relative to that for clearly diagnostic information regarding incumbent competence – report (a) – speaks directly to the sophistication of benchmark use.

Figure 7 presents the findings for the 750 participants who completed Experiment 8. Figure 7(A)–(B) plots the distribution of reports chosen by game design. The results reveal a clear preference for comparative performance summaries. Looking at the individual selections in Figure 7(A), the report on the relative gap in the two workers' averages is chosen as or more frequently than the incumbent's report in both games and is the modal choice among subjects assigned to the

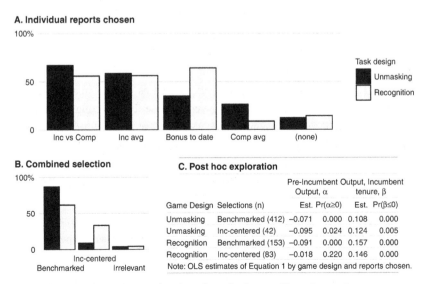

Figure 7 Pursuing benchmarked cues, Experiment 8

unmasking game (34 percent). Turning to participants' joint selections in Figure 7 (B), a large majority of participants in the recognition arm (63 percent) opted for a comparison, choosing either the incumbent *and* comparator averages separately or the benchmarked report directly. In the unmasking arm, nearly every participant (87 percent) sought a comparison. In stark contrast, less than 10 percent of participants in the unmasking arm and 33 percent in the recognition arm chose an incumbent-focused set of reports (i.e., only the incumbent's average without also selecting the contrast or comparator's average).[51] These results suggest that benchmarking is a consciously favored mode of evaluation.

The preference for a benchmark is clear, but the pattern of information seeking differs by game. Those assigned to the unmasking arm were more likely to seek comparative reports, and the difference in the distributions is significant ($\chi_2^2 = 70.3$, $p < 0.001$). We suspect that this reflects the simplicity of the recognition game: view incumbent performance in isolation (in weeks 9–16) and then vote. The reports may appear less valuable in this context. In contrast, participants assigned to the unmasking game confront a genuine extraction problem: infer their incumbent's competence from a stream of data obscured by an exogenous disturbance. The necessity of judging performance amid uncertainty may elevate the utility of the summary reports. In this context, nearly everyone sought comparative information.

Perhaps the pattern reflects an undue pressure to select two reports. If participants saw the choice of *up to two* reports as a mandate, rather than a genuine choice, the results might inflate the percentage "seeking" comparative information. If this were true, participants who chose to view the incumbent's report should select their second report at random. Yet the choice is systematic ($\chi_3^2 = 156.1, p < 0.001$ and $\chi_3^2 = 58.5, p < 0.001$ for the unmasking and recognition arms respectively).

Finally, Figure 7(C) offers a post hoc exploration of benchmarking behavior in the reappointment decision by the type of reports chosen. Here, we estimate Equation 1 by study design, comparing the responses to performance among those selecting benchmarked comparisons versus those few selecting incumbent-focused reports. In the unmasking game, we see clear evidence of benchmark comparison in both groups with no distinction in the magnitude of the parameter estimates. However, we see no evidence of benchmarking among those selecting incumbent-centric reports in the recognition game. Here, the response is strictly to the incumbent's performance and ignores the performance of the comparator. Whether this is a selection effect or an indication of the role that quality benchmarks, or quality heuristics, play in retrospective voting is a focus of Experiment 9.

---

[51] Only one in twenty-five choose strictly irrelevant reports (neither the incumbent's average nor the comparison) – far lower than the 33 percent we would expect by chance.

6.2 Experiment 9: Does Information Matter?

Whereas the goal in Experiment 8 was to observe information-seeking behavior, Experiment 9 assesses the effect of different performance cues on the integration-appraisal process. To this end, we replicate Experiment 8 with the key exception that we randomly assign participants to a performance report, rather than permitting them to choose.[52] We expose participants to one of three summary reports:

(a) Incumbent's average production
(b) The difference between the incumbent and comparator's averages
(c) Bonus earned to date (a control)

The assigned report appears on screen immediately prior to voting on the incumbent's reappointment. If benchmark processing is a default evaluative heuristic, the benchmark response should persist in the presence of non-benchmarked reports.[53]

Figure 8 plots the estimated response to factory performance before and after the incumbent's arrival ($\hat{\alpha}$ and $\hat{\beta}$) by treatment report and game design for 1,376 participants.[54] Across all treatments in the unmasking game, we find a response to both the comparator's performance in the first eight weeks (black squares) and the factory total in the second eight weeks (gray circles). As in Experiments

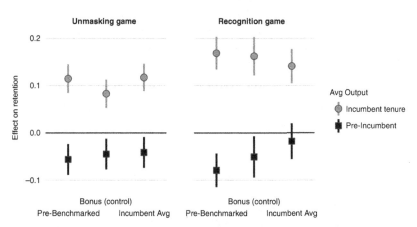

Figure 8 Quality cues may limit benchmarking in simple tasks, Experiment 9

---

[52] As in Experiment 8, we randomly assign subjects to play the unmasking or recognition game with probabilities 1/3 and 2/3, respectively.

[53] For this experiment, we registered tests of retrospective voting ($\beta > 0$) and benchmarking ($\alpha < 0$), and moderation of these relationships by the performance cues, here: https://doi.org/10.17605/OSF.IO/NGCPX.

[54] Estimates for the full sample by treatment arm are given in Table 6.

5, 7, and 8 (unmasking arm), the results are consistent with the benchmarking theory and contrary to blind retrospection and rational discounting. On their face, assignment to the pre-benchmarked *and* incumbent-average reports strengthens the response to both streams, but these shifts, relative to an uninformative bonus-to-date condition, are not statistically significant.

In the recognition arm, participants assigned to the control report benchmark the incumbent against the irrelevant comparator. This is consistent with the findings from Experiments 6 and 8 (recognition arm). Interestingly, the benchmark response is greater in the pre-benchmarked report condition, but the increase is not significant. Most importantly, participants assigned to the only relevant report – the incumbent's average output – do not gauge the incumbent's performance in relation to the comparator, and the difference relative to the benchmark report condition is statistically significant $(Pr(\alpha_{Inc} \geq \alpha_{Bench}) = 0.013)$. This follows the same pattern observed in the post hoc analysis of Experiment 8. However, the drop in response to the comparator relative to the control condition is not statistically significant $(Pr(\alpha_{Inc} \geq \alpha_{Bonus}) = 0.128)$. Curiously, the response to the incumbent's performance attenuates $(\hat{\beta}_{Inc} - \hat{\beta}_{Bench} = -0.028)$, though not significantly $(Pr(\beta_{Inc} \leq \beta_{Bench}) = 0.148)$.

Overall, the results from Experiment 9 highlight the persistence of benchmarking strategies in the integration-appraisal process. That assignment to pre-benchmarked performance reports does not amplify the comparative response relative to the control condition suggests that benchmarking is a default mode of processing in the presence of interdependent or confounded performance outcomes. Finally, we find limited evidence that treating participants with clearly diagnostic performance information (i.e., the incumbent's performance average) reduces the propensity to benchmark, at least relative to rates of benchmarking in the presence of a pre-benchmarked report.

6.3 Experiment 10: Do Voters Choose Quality Benchmarks?

Experiments 10 and 11 jointly address questions about the "sophistication" of benchmark use. Whereas findings from Experiment 8 reveal a stark preference for comparative performance cues over more relevant incumbent-centered cues, it is unclear if individuals blindly pursue comparative information or if they seek to identify the most relevant comparisons. Experiment 10, therefore, allows participants to select a point of comparison prior to voting on their incumbent. Across a range of available benchmarks, do individuals gravitate toward more relevant referents?

The design of Experiment 10 starts with the baseline game, wherein participants observe the incumbent's performance for sixteen weeks before voting on
reappointment. However, we strip the instructions of any reference to the
parameters of possible worker types, though we do note that potential replacements are drawn "from the same pool ... and will arrive with the same
training."[55] Whereas *all* prior experiments in this Element instruct participants
that underlying types follow a uniform distribution ranging from 950 to 1,450
units per week, Experiment 10 presents no a priori standard against which to
appraise a worker's performance. Instead, we allow participants to select among
five possible benchmarks of varying quality:

> As you evaluate [the incumbent] you may wish to review factory perform-
> ance records for reference. You may select one (1) of the reports below,
> giving the average weekly output for different workers in your department in
> recent years.

- Lowest producing worker
- Worker in the bottom 25%
- Average worker in your department
- Worker in the top 25%
- Highest producing worker

To allow for the possibility that the timing of the opportunity to acquire
benchmark information matters, participants are randomly assigned to make
their selections after eight or sixteen weeks of the game.

This design clearly pushes subjects to compare the incumbent's revealed
performance against the chosen standard. The goal, however, is not to identify
benchmarking behavior but rather to see if participants, when compelled to
benchmark, can identify a suitable basis for appraisal. Given that the replacement worker would be drawn from the "same pool" as the incumbent, the
"Average worker" is the most appropriate choice and the historical high/low
the least appropriate.[56]

Figure 9(A) presents the selections among the full sample as well as by the
timing of the selection. A clear plurality of participants (43 percent) chose the
historical average as their referent. There appears to be a slight preference for
"aspirational" benchmarks, with 29 percent choosing a worker in the top
quartile and better than one in ten (13 percent) choosing the highest producing

---

[55] Experiment 10 instructions still identify and explain the normal distribution of weekly output.

[56] As the goal of this experiment is exploratory, we registered three research questions, concerning
whether the distribution of choices was systematic, the "average" report was the modal choice,
and the timing of the information search opportunity affected the choice distribution. See https://
doi.org/10.17605/OSF.IO/93JU2.

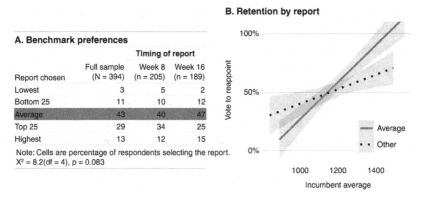

Figure 9 Selecting quality benchmarks by timing, Experiment 10

worker on record. Critically, the distribution of preferences is systematic ($\chi_4^2 = 207.0, p < 0.001$) and unrelated to the incumbent's actual performance ($F_4 = 1.031, p = 0.391$). We see that the preference for the historical average is nominally higher when the reports are offered immediately prior to the vote (47 percent vs. 40 percent), when the "gravity" of the information for the vote decision may be highest. However, we cannot rule out the independence of timing and selection of report ($\chi_4^2 = 8.1, p = 0.088$).

Turning to Figure 9(B), we note that participants were responsive to their incumbent's performance. In the absence of even an implicit guide to appraisal in the instructions, a 100-unit increase in average yield raises the probability of reappointment by 0.10. We also observe in post hoc analysis that the response to incumbent performance (solid line) is significantly higher among those who chose the "average" report than among those who did not (dotted line). Given that exposure to benchmarks was observed rather than manipulated, we cannot say whether this difference reflects the quality of the benchmark or a selection effect.

Sophisticated benchmark seeking and processing may not be necessary to promote the accountability function of elections. Media coverage of national economic performance, for example, is often "pre-benchmarked" (e.g., Kayser and Peress, 2012) and may focus heavily on peer economies (Park, 2019). Yet we find that a strong plurality of Experiment 10 participants identified the most appropriate basis for comparison among a range of possibilities. On the one hand, we cannot take this as evidence of especially sophisticated behavior, and we note that the flipside of our finding is that a majority – across timing conditions – failed to choose the most appropriate referent. On the other hand, Experiment 10 participants were the first to complete our game without *any* upfront guidelines for appraisal. This may mitigate concerns about something like "blind benchmarking," especially in information environments with multiple referents available.

6.4 Experiment 11: Can Voters Adjust for a Bad Benchmark?

For better or worse, participants in Experiments 5–10 saw signs of competence in distinctions between the performances of similarly situated peers. Our final experiment turns this problem on its head, challenging participants to instead see signs of competence in the similarity of performances between the incumbent and a comparator with distinct advantages or disadvantages. Without other bases for appraisal, can individuals prone to differentiate see parity as a clear sign of competence?

The logic of the design is that, if voters are "sophisticated benchmarkers," then they ought to recognize and adjust for exogenous, and therefore irrelevant, influences on the benchmark. As an analogy, consider the economic voter who evaluates an incumbent by comparing their country's economic performance to that of a salient peer economy. If that voter becomes aware that the peer country has been struck by a large-scale natural disaster, then any perceived difference between the countries' performances should be adjusted for this "shock" to the comparator's circumstances. Put differently, does the voter perceive the similarity between performance in their country and a peer country amid objective shock as a sign of incumbent incompetence?

Experiment 11 utilizes a multi-stream design in which participants simultaneously view separate streams of incumbent and comparator output without interference for sixteen weeks. As with the prior experiment, we strip the instructions of any reference to the distribution of worker types. Instead, we explicitly identify the comparator as a historically average performer but note that, with the incumbent's arrival, the comparator will have to move to a machine that is:

- considerably slower and less efficient;
- equivalent (control); or,
- considerably faster and more efficient.

We assign subjects at random to one of these conditions. In this design, differences in machine efficiency constitute an exogenous shock to the comparator's circumstances. Rather than randomize expected worker types, we set them equal across treatments and participants, and incumbent and comparator output are random draws from the same distribution

Table 5 Reappointment by comparator's "shocked" standard, Experiment 11

	DV: Vote to reappoint incumbent			
	Full sample		Small gap	
	(1)	(2)	(3)	(4)
Comparator's new machine:				
Slower than incumbent's	0.007	0.008		−0.004
	(0.039)	(0.038)		(0.043)
Faster than incumbent's	0.076*	0.071*		0.114**
	(0.039)	(0.038)		(0.042)
Incumbent's average		0.130**	0.131**	
		(0.032)	(0.032)	
Comparator's average		−0.181**	−0.182**	
		(0.032)	(0.032)	
Constant	0.566**	1.174*	1.197*	0.562**
	(0.027)	(0.538)	(0.538)	(0.029)
Observations	918	918	918	774

Note. OLS estimates with standard errors in parentheses. Worker averages scaled in 100s of units. $^*p < 0.05$; $^{**}p < 0.01$, 1-tailed.

($Y_t \sim N(1,200,200)$). Our aim is to test whether participants respond to the similarity of performance in a way that adjusts for the "shock" to comparator output. Do participants see competence if their incumbent matches a systematically advantaged comparator, and do they punish incumbents for tracking the performance of a disadvantaged comparator?

Model 1 of Table 5 presents OLS estimates of the effect of the shocked comparator cue on incumbent reappointment for the 918 participants who completed Experiment 11.[57] Here, we see a reward for an incumbent who produces at levels similar to a comparator operating on a more efficient machine relative to a comparator operating on an equivalent machine. Assignment to this condition increases the probability of reappointment by about 0.08, and the bump is statistically significant ($p = 0.027$, 1-tailed). However, we find no reflexive punishment for an incumbent who matches a comparator on a slower machine. That said, we cannot reject the independence of the vote and the shock cue treatment ($F_{2,915} = 2.219, p = 0.109$).

---

[57] The expectations tested in this paragraph are registered here: https://doi.org/10.17605/OSF.IO/5KRPJ.

Although the baseline types for each worker are equivalent in expectation, the revealed difference in incumbent and comparator averages ranged from −259 to 198 units per week with a standard deviation of 71. Thus, at the extreme end of the distributions, participants might reasonably see distinction between the workers. In this case, the relative scores may not be doing the work we think they are. Model 4, then, focuses on the subsample for whom the absolute gap between incumbent and comparator averages is less than 100 units per week.[58] Here, the response to the positive shock nearly doubles and we can reject the independence of the shock treatment and vote choice ($F_{2,771} = 4.764, p = 0.009$).

Models 2 and 3 leverage the random differences in incumbent and comparator performance and offer a post hoc test of benchmark processing. Again, we see clear evidence that participants reward incumbents for outperforming a referent. Like many of the prior studies, we see this even where we make clear that the comparison is not a good one. On the other hand, the Experiment 11 design provides no other bases for appraisal. Moreover, we see the clear and strong comparison even though the relative performance gap is much smaller than in prior studies.

6.5 Summary

Starting from the premise that the tendency to benchmark performance may reflect a heuristic process, in this section we investigated voters' capacity to discriminate amongst benchmarks of varying quality. Experiment 8 revealed that our participants have a "taste" for benchmarking, even when the available benchmarks are irrelevant and clearly diagnostic information is equally available. The results of Experiment 9 suggest the benchmarking tendency is automatic and robust: Exposure to pre-benchmarked performance cues does not enhance it, while exposure to the most relevant performance information (generally) does not diminish it. Experiment 10 provides suggestive evidence that many − but by no means all − voters can discriminate amongst benchmarks of varying quality. Finally, Experiment 11 offers mixed evidence of a capacity to recognize and adjust for "bad" benchmarks. Our participants reward an incumbent who performs to the standard of a comparator who enjoys systematic − but irrelevant − advantages; conversely, there is no sign that our participants make a similar adjustment when benchmarking incumbents to disadvantaged comparators.

---

[58] Estimates and substantive conclusions are robust to other cutoffs.

7 Conclusion

The unifying thread across conventional models of retrospective voting is the idea that voters' evaluations of the state of the world motivate their decisions to reelect or replace elected officials. Fundamental to this behavior, we have argued, is the integration-appraisal task (cf. Downs, 1957; Achen and Bartels, 2016). Voters encounter information relevant to their government's performance across the timeline of electoral politics and must somehow integrate these streams of information and register an appraisal of government performance. Yet observational studies of retrospective voting do not convincingly isolate the integration-appraisal task and nearly all experimental studies short-circuit at least one of its phases. How – and how effectively – do voters make sense of government performance?

We developed in this Element an abstract experimental framework for studying retrospective voting that challenges our participants to integrate and appraise performance information *themselves*. Where past research simplified the informational context of retrospective voting, we confront our "voters" with the inherent complexity of performance evaluation in environments that provide manifold, and sometimes confounded, indicators of performance over time. The flexibility of our framework allowed us to field eleven experiments testing a wide range of fundamental claims in retrospective voting theory. Moreover, as we argued in Section 2, the abstract nature of our framework increased leverage over the hypotheses under scrutiny and enhanced our capacity to make theory-driven generalizations.

In this concluding section, we first review our principal findings and their theoretical and normative significance. Next, we reflect on what we have gained through our novel emphasis on the integration-appraisal task. Finally, we identify future research directions suggested by our study.

7.1 Retrospective Voting and Democracy

Are voters capable of integrating and appraising streams of performance information in such a way that rewards good performance and punishes poor performance? Yes. Exposed to a stream of performance information, the participants in Experiment 1 retained their incumbent workers in direct proportion to their quality. In the absence of the simplifications typically afforded participants in retrospective voting experiments – performance summaries and accompanying appraisals – our "voters" competently integrated over workers' weekly output and formed evaluations tied to their interests (i.e., maximization of their post-game payout). Experiment 2 showed that this tendency was not compromised by higher levels of variability in performance (at least in the context of the relatively straightforward baseline game). Experiments 5 and 7 revealed our participants' ability to deploy a strategy of benchmarking to extract incumbent quality from streams of performance information confounded with spillover from irrelevant comparators. A sizable plurality of participants in Experiment 10, given a choice among possible performance benchmarks to aid their decision-making, favored the optimal standard for comparison. Experiment 11, finally, suggested a capacity to use benchmarks thoughtfully – specifically, to apply benchmarking in a way that adjusts for random perturbations in comparator performance that are irrelevant to an assessment of incumbent quality.

Do voters manage the integration-appraisal task without error or bias? Clearly, they do not. While Experiment 1 showed that performance matters, retention behavior was suboptimal: Above-average workers were not uniformly retained, those below average were not uniformly replaced, and perfectly average workers were more likely to be retained than replaced. The latter finding, an incumbency bias, suggests our participants were risk-averse: Given the parameters of the game, expectations for perfectly average incumbent workers are equivalent to those for replacement workers – thus, our participants ought to have retained and replaced equal numbers of average incumbents. Experiment 4 revealed a second bias, in favor of recent performance – a finding that was corroborated in post hoc analyses of Experiments 1 and 2.[59] Evidence for a third bias – negativity bias – was more equivocal. Experiment 3 was purpose-built to detect a particular manifestation of negativity bias, one reflected in differential responsiveness to performances that are a fixed distance above and below a clear reference point (the "historical average" for all workers). This test produces a striking result: Not only does negative information *not* outweigh positive information, the impact of positive information on retention decisions is nearly three times the impact of negative information. Yet, as we argue in Section 4, these results are open to an alternative interpretation: If we assume that appraisal precedes integration in the over-time evaluation of performance, then our results are readily reconciled with the existence of negativity bias. Further, post hoc analyses of Experiments 1 and 2 are consistent with negativity bias, though the test of asymmetry misses conventional significance thresholds.

---

[59] In isolation, the impact of recency in Experiment 4 need not be interpreted as a problematic "bias." As participants in this experiment were not advised that worker performance was stable over time, they may have inferred, sensibly, that later weeks of production were more diagnostic of future performance than early weeks. Yet we observe a similar recency effect in Experiment 1 and 2, which did advise that worker performance "typically does not change over time." We therefore infer that the relative impact of recent performance does not reflect the belief that it is more informative.

Evidence that benchmarking pervades retrospective evaluation must also be carefully weighed in arriving at a normative assessment of our results. As noted, voters should be praised for benchmarking to extract estimates of incumbent quality from confounded streams of performance information, as our participants did in Experiments 5 and 7. In Experiment 6, however, benchmarking leads them astray: In this "recognition" design, which offers participants an unobstructed look at incumbent performance, the comparator's performance is an irrelevant distraction. And our participants *were* distracted: They were less likely to reappoint their incumbent as the (irrelevant) comparator's performance improved. The finding suggests that a salient benchmark is hard to resist. Experiment 8, furthermore, revealed our participants had a "taste" for benchmarking, with the vast majority choosing to acquire comparative performance information from a list of indicators that also included information that was perfectly diagnostic of performance: Their incumbent's average production. Experiment 9 showed that the provision of the incumbent's performance average does not consistently weaken the tendency to benchmark: Whereas exposure to the incumbent's average neutralized benchmarking among participants assigned to the recognition game, provision of this information had no effect among those playing the unmasking game. Strong as the attraction to benchmarks may be, it may be more easily undone in settings, like the recognition game, where the salient benchmarks are clearly irrelevant.

We also note the flipside of two encouraging observations regarding our participants' approach to benchmarking. Given a choice of benchmarks in Experiment 10, a plurality of participants made the optimal selection – but a *majority* did not, choosing to review, instead, the performance of the best or worst workers, or of a worker in the top or bottom quartile. And while participants in Experiment 11 ably adjusted their use of benchmarks for a positive, but random, perturbation to a comparator's performance, there is no sign whatsoever they applied the same logic when considering a negatively "shocked" comparator.

What image of the retrospective voter emerges, then, from this long list of findings? Taken together, we observe a voter who is clearly lacking the unconstrained, comprehensive decision-making rationality imagined in some formal accounts of voting behavior (e.g., Enelow and Hinich, 1984). Equally, however, the participants in our studies do not conform to the worst fears inspired by accounts of blind retrospection, which suggest a voter who indiscriminately attributes to government all manner of victories and defeats, both personal and collective (e.g., Achen and Bartels, 2016). Indeed, if the test of rationality is an ability to distinguish the sources of one's welfare from exogenous and uncontrollable influences, then the participants in our

Table 6 Benchmark processing in multi-stream games

Study	Design (n)	Response to production Pre-incumbent ($F_{pre,i}$)		Incumbent tenure ($F_{post,i}$)	
		$\hat{\alpha}$	$Pr(\alpha \geq 0)$	$\hat{\beta}$	$Pr(\beta \leq 0)$
5	Unmasking (819)	−0.093	< 0.001	0.135	< 0.001
6	Recognition (368)	−0.055	< 0.001	0.123	< 0.001
7	Unmasking (550)	−0.114	< 0.001	0.158	< 0.001
8	Unmasking arm (173)	−0.129	< 0.001	0.151	< 0.001
	Recognition arm (217)	−0.065	< 0.001	0.153	< 0.001
9	Unmasking arm (894)	−0.138	< 0.001	0.192	< 0.001
	Recognition arm (182)	−0.047	< 0.001	0.156	< 0.001
11	Dual stream (918)	−0.182	< 0.001	0.131	< 0.001

Note. OLS estimates of Equation 1 by study and game design. Each regresses the vote to reappoint the Incumbent on factory performance. Output scaled in 100s of units and intercepts suppressed for simplicity. Note that coefficients are not directly comparable as the number of workers and variance of output differs across experiments.

experiments have passed with flying colors. As we suggest in Section 6, an extreme version of blind retrospection suggests that the impact of exogenous performance information on incumbent retention in our multi-stream games should be positive: that is, participants should reward their incumbent for performance that is clearly not attributable to the incumbent's efforts. As shown in Table 6, however, across all six multi-stream experiments, the relevant coefficient (i.e., $\hat{\alpha}$, the effect of factory production prior to the incumbent's arrival) is negative. Notably, in this regard our findings would seem to contradict those of Huber et al. (2012), whose most striking finding was the positive responsiveness of participants in their incentivized experimental game to a "lottery" affecting their payouts that was plainly unrelated to their allocator's performance.

The retrospective voter emerging from our study consistently makes reasonable – if not exclusive – use of the information regarding incumbent performance to which they are exposed, rewarding and punishing their workers in direct proportion to their productivity. The voter autonomously formulates appraisals of worker performance that are strongly correlated with their underlying interests (in maximizing worker productivity and, thus, payouts), even as they fail to apply the optimum rule for doing so. The voter is apt to rely on readily available benchmarks to formulate their appraisals, which, in some conditions, has the happy side effect of helping their retention decisions hew more closely to the quality of the incumbent's performance. Unfortunately, the voter also tends to rely on available benchmarks when they are irrelevant or misleading – sometimes even when perfectly diagnostic information is available – and they are more likely than not to make a suboptimal selection when offered a choice of benchmark. The voter's psychology is also subject to a set of distortions (incumbency and recency bias certainly, negativity bias possibly) that bedevil human decision-making in many settings.[60]

In terms of classic models of public opinion and voting behavior, our image of the retrospective voter is best aligned with the "low-information rationality" perspective exemplified by Popkin (1991) and Sniderman et al. (1991). Lau and Redlawsk (2006) – in a study of political information processing that resonates methodologically and theoretically with ours – characterize this perspective as "a view of humans as cognitively limited information processors" (p. 14). In contrast to more rationalist perspectives, this approach portrays a voter who makes "decisions in a much more 'intuitive' (i.e. less formal and calculating) manner" (p. 14). Such a voter is "guided by two competing motivations: the desire to make a *good* decision and the desire to make an *easy* decision" (p. 14; emphasis in original). The retrospective voter in our study seemingly strives to inform their decisions with the most relevant information; at the same time, they rely too heavily on a set of cognitive strategies – especially benchmarking – that are useful in many settings but generally lead to suboptimal outcomes in the context of our experiments. Still, the manifest limitations of our participants were not outright hindrances to accountability. With some exceptions, our voters managed, across easy and difficult tasks, to reward good performance and punish bad performance.

---

[60] While we have termed them "biases" in this study, these phenomena are not universally incompatible with rationality: for instance, recent information may actually be more informative than earlier information in some settings (Healy and Lenz, 2014). In the present study, however, these decision-making tendencies can only bias the average participant away from their maximum possible payout.

7.2 Integration-Appraisal and the Study
of Retrospective Voting

This study is premised on the idea that a more convincing experimental test of retrospective voting theory requires a design that does not short-circuit the integration-appraisal task – a design that allows participants to autonomously combine and evaluate performance information. What have we gained by studying retrospective voting in this fashion?

First, to state the obvious, the principal gain is a *more direct and robust test of retrospective voting theory.* We now have clear, experimental evidence not only that citizens *apply* evaluations of performance to vote decisions – as diverse existing experimental studies already confirm – but that citizens can and do integrate and appraise performance information while forming performance evaluations. To be sure, our new evidence would not count for much if the integration-appraisal task were trivial or obvious – but the task is neither of these things. As we describe in Section 5, the existing scholarship's expectations concerning integration run the gamut from highly rational discounting strategies to highly arbitrary and indiscriminate retrospection. As regards appraisal, the retrospective voting literature is mostly silent, save for research on the role of global benchmarks in economic voting, which has so far reached mixed conclusions (Kayser and Peress, 2012; Arel-Bundock et al., 2019).

Second, we have introduced and shed light on questions that are difficult or impossible to study outside of designs that allow integration and appraisal to unfold "naturally." We have studied how variability – an attribute of performance rendered completely invisible in the "short-circuited" designs – affects retrospective evaluation: While variability doesn't seem to matter in the context of the baseline game (Experiment 2), it weakens responsiveness to performance information in a more informationally complex setting (Experiment 5). Most significantly, our various evidence regarding the pervasive impact of benchmarks on performance evaluation (Experiments 5–9, 11) powerfully demonstrates the role of informational context in shaping the appraisal process. Likewise, in comparing the results of Experiments 1–3, in analysis that was incidental to our investigation of negativity bias, we find that highlighting a particular performance standard (i.e., a historical average) roughly doubles the effect of performance on incumbent retention. This gives some sense of the scale of the consequences that flow from the short-circuiting of the appraisal process in previous experimental studies of retrospective voting.

Third, we unearthed new complexity in retrospective voting by highlighting the potential importance of the sequence in which integration and appraisal proceed. We happened upon the question accidentally: As we discuss in

Section 4, our design for studying negativity bias was premised on the idea that performance information is first integrated and then appraised. Given that premise, the results of Experiment 3 contradict the expectation of negativity bias. However, given an alternative premise – that appraisal precedes integration – the results comport easily with the existence of negativity bias. The obvious, but potentially important, lesson is that theoretical work on the processing of performance information into retrospective evaluations must consider explicitly how integration and appraisal interact over time.

7.3 Next Steps in the Study of Retrospective Voting

Ultimately, we hope that our findings will contribute to the advancement of retrospective voting theory. We have identified clear tendencies in the integration-appraisal process, some of which directly contradict or challenge baseline assumptions of conventional models. We cannot claim to have "solved" the integration-appraisal process or to have shown that voters in real-world elections follow the tendencies we identified in this Element. The results should nonetheless put theorists, experimentalists, and observationalists into conversation, and there are several areas we are keen to explore.

A number of specific research directions flow immediately from the findings in this Element. Our findings are notably mixed regarding the significance to retrospective voting of variability in incumbent performance. As there is scarce evidence in existing literature on this question, along with sound theoretical reasons for suspecting variability may matter, more research – whether in the context of an abstract design such as ours or any manner of experimental or observational research – is needed.[61] Equally pressing is further experimental work on negativity bias in retrospective voting. To our knowledge, our studies on this topic are unique and, as we have emphasized, their implications are equivocal. The next step is a design that cleanly identifies asymmetry in performance whether appraisal follows *or* precedes integration. Lastly, while we have provided the most evidence in regard to the role of benchmarking in performance evaluation, the results of Experiment 11 are tantalizing. Why do our participants adjust for a positively, but not a negatively, perturbed benchmark? Notably, this result contradicts expectations of negativity bias – and, unlike the results in Section 4, very convincingly so.

More generally, our study makes a case for much more theoretical and empirical attention to the role of, what we might term, "appraisal cues" in the formation of performance evaluations. As noted in Section 7.2, apart from

---

[61] Quinn and Woolley's (2001) observational study is the exception; however, we are unaware of any existing experimental studies of variability's impact on retrospective voting.

limited work on benchmarking (e.g., Park, 2019), this problem is generally neglected in the existing literature, though our findings on the impact of salient benchmarks suggest the availability of appraisal cues could exert a powerful influence on the nature of retrospective performance evaluation. Lack of attention to appraisal cues may reflect the overriding dominance of economic voting in the retrospective voting literature. Performance information in the economic domain is generally accompanied by a host of prominent appraisal cues: Reports of annual change in unemployment and gross domestic product (GDP), for example, implicitly suggest the monthly or annual baseline as a standard of performance, and scholars have generally (though not uniformly) imported these implicit standards of evaluation into their analyses. In other domains, however, standards of appraisal may be much less clear and much more contentious. In a study of how Americans interpreted the progress of the Iraq War, Gaines et al. (2007) describe the context of performance evaluation in a way we find generally instructive: "politics does not provide common standards or criteria by which citizens can attribute meaning to given facts. People cannot turn to a manual to determine if an additional 50 troop casualties during the past month represents a big, moderate, or small loss. They either make the interpretations themselves or let others – partisan politicians, for instance – do it for them" (p. 959).

Finally, the interaction of processes of integration and appraisal over time also strikes us as an exciting area for future study. A natural point of departure is suggested by our alternative interpretation of the results of Experiment 3, which is premised on the idea that appraisal precedes integration. As a generalization regarding performance evaluation, what would the primacy of appraisal imply? If we could substitute "affect" for "appraisal" in the previous sentence, then the generalization would fit neatly with prominent theoretical models that assume the valence of our immediate, unconscious emotional responses to information drive much of our political attitudes and behavior (Lodge and Taber, 2013; Pérez, 2016). At the same time, such models are not obviously compatible with the strong evidence of recency bias in Experiment 4 (see also Stiers et al., 2020). To reconcile these seemingly discrepant patterns, we might highlight a critical difference between Experiments 3 and 4: While a strong appraisal cue was provided (by necessity) in Experiment 3, no such cue was provided in Experiment 4. The implication is that the primacy of appraisal is conditional on the availability of a standard for appraisal at the moment performance information is encountered. This is a novel hypothesis that is ready for testing.

References

Achen, C. H. & Bartels, L. M. (2016). *Democracy for Realists*. Princeton, NJ: Princeton University Press.

Alcañiz, I. & Hellwig, T. (2011). Who's to Blame? The Distribution of Responsibility in Developing Democracies. *British Journal of Political Science* 41(2): 389–411.

Alesina, A. & Rosenthal, H. (1995). *Partisan Politics, Divided Government, and the Economy*. Cambridge: Cambridge University Press.

Angrist, J. D. & Pischke, J. (2015). *Mastering 'Metrics*. Princeton, NJ: Princeton University Press.

Arel-Bundock, V., Blais, A., & Dassonneville, R. (2019). Do Voters Benchmark Economic Performance? *British Journal of Political Science* 51(1): 1–13.

Ashraf, N., Berry, J., & Shapiro, J. M. (2010). Can Higher Prices Stimulate Product Use? Evidence from a Field Experiment in Zambia. *American Economic Review* 100(5): 2383–2413.

Aytaç, S. E. (2018). Relative Economic Performance and the Incumbent Vote: A Reference Point Theory. *Journal of Politics* 80(1): 16–29.

Banerjee, A. V. (2005). "New Development Economics" and the Challenge to Theory. *Economic and Political Weekly* 40(40): 4340–4344.

Banerjee, A. V. (2020). Field Experiments and the Practice of Economics. *American Economic Review* 110(7): 1937–1951.

Banerjee, A. V. & Duflo, E. (2009). The Experimental Approach to Development Economics. *Annual Review of Economics* 1: 151–178.

Banerjee, A. V. & Duflo, E. (2011). *Poor Economics*. New York: PublicAffairs.

Baumeister, R. F., Bratslavsky, E., Finkenauer, C., & Vohs, K. D. (2001). Bad Is Stronger Than Good. *Review of General Psychology* 5(4): 323–370.

Berry, C. R. & Howell, W. G. (2007). Accountability and Local Elections: Rethinking Retrospective Voting. *Journal of Politics* 69(3): 844–858.

Besley, T. & Case, A. (1995). Incumbent Behavior: Vote-Seeking, Tax-Setting, and Yardstick Competition. *American Economic Review* 85(1): 25–45.

Bhandari, A., Larreguy, H., & Marshall, J. (2023). Able and Mostly Willing: An Empirical Anatomy of Information's Effect on Voter-Driven Accountability in Senegal. *American Journal of Political Science*. https://doi.org/10.1111/ajps.12591.

Bloom, H. S. & Price, H. D. (1975). Voter Response to Short-Run Economic Conditions: The Asymmetric Effect of Prosperity and Recession. *American Political Science Review* 69(4): 1240–1254.

Boudreau, C. (2009). Closing the Gap: When Do Cues Eliminate Differences between Sophisticated and Unsophisticated Citizens? *Journal of Politics* 71 (3): 964–976.

Brutger, R., Kertzer, J., Renshon, J., & Weiss, C. (2022). *Abstraction in Experimental Design: Testing the Tradeoffs* (Elements in Experimental Political Science). Cambridge: Cambridge University Press.

Campbell, D. T. & Stanley, J. C. (1963). *Experimental and Quasi-experimental Designs for Research*. Boston, MA: Houghton Mifflin.

Campello, D. & Zucco, C. (2016). Presidential Success and the World Economy. *Journal of Politics*, 78(2): 589–602.

Cartwright, N. (2007). *Hunting Causes and Using Them*. Cambridge: Cambridge University Press.

Casey, L. S., Chandler, J., Levine, A. S., Proctor, A., & Strolovitch, D. Z. (2017). Intertemporal Differences among MTurk Workers: Time-Based Sample Variations and Implications for Online Data Collection. *Sage Open* 7(2).

Charbonneau, É. & Ryzin, G. G. V. (2015). Benchmarks and Citizen Judgments of Local Government Performance: Findings from a Survey Experiment. *Public Management Review* 17(2): 288–304.

Clinton, J. D. & Grissom, J. A. (2015). Public Information, Public Learning and Public Opinion: Democratic Accountability in Education Policy. *Journal of Public Policy* 35(3): 355–385.

Cohen, J. E. (2020). Relative Unemployment, Political Information, and the Job Approval Ratings of State Governors and Legislatures. *State Politics & Policy Quarterly* 20(4): 437–461.

Cohen, J. & Dupas, P. (2010). Free Distribution or Cost-Sharing? Evidence from a Randomized Malaria Prevention Experiment. *The Quarterly Journal of Economics* 125(1): 1–45.

Cole, S., Healy, A., & Werker, E. (2012). Do Voters Demand Responsive Governments? Evidence from Indian Disaster Relief. *Journal of Development Economics* 97(2): 167–181.

Davis, C. & Mobarek, A. (2020). The Challenges of Scaling Effective Interventions: A Path Forward for Research and Policy. *World Development* 127: 104817.

Downs, A. (1957). *An Economic Theory of Democracy*. New York: Harper & Row.

Druckman, J. (2022). *Experimental Thinking: A Primer on Social Science Experiments*. Cambridge: Cambridge University Press.

Duch, R. M. & Stevenson, R. (2008). *The Economic Vote: How Political and Economic Institutions Condition Election Results*. New York: Cambridge University Press.

Duch, R. M. & Stevenson, R. (2010). The Global Economy, Competency, and the Economic Vote. *Journal of Politics* 72(1): 105–123.

Ebeid, M. & Rodden, J. (2006). Economic Geography and Economic Voting: Evidence from the US States. *British Journal of Political Science* 36(3) 527–547.

Enelow, J. M. & Hinich, M. J. (1984). *The Spatial Theory of Voting: An Introduction*. New York: Cambridge University Press.

Ferejohn, J. (1986). Incumbent Performance and Electoral Control. *Public Choice* 50(1/3): 5–25.

Festinger, L. (1954). A Theory of Social Comparison Processes. *Human Relations* 7(2): 117–140.

Findley, M. G., Kikuta, K., & Denly, M. (2021). External Validity. *Annual Review of Political Science* 24: 365–393.

Fiorina, M. (1981). *Retrospective Voting in American National Elections*. New Haven, CT: Yale University Press.

Fiorina, M. P. & Plott, C. R. (1978). Committee Decisions under Majority Rule: An Experimental Study. *American Political Science Review* 72(2): 575–598.

Fisher, R. A. (1935). *The Design of Experiments*. Edinburgh: Oliver & Boyd.

Fowler, A. & Montagnes, B. P. (2015). College Football, Elections, and False-Positive Results in Observational Research. *Proceedings of the National Academy of Sciences* 112(45): 13800–13804.

Gaines, B. J., Kuklinski, J. H., Quirk, P. J., Peyton, B., & Verkuilen, J. (2007). Same Facts, Different Interpretations: Partisan Motivation and Opinion on Iraq. *Journal of Politics* 69(4): 957–974.

Gastorf, J. W. & Suls, J. (1978). Performance Evaluation via Social Comparison: Performance Similarity versus Related-Attribute Similarity. *Social Psychology* 41(4): 297–305.

Gelineau, F. & Remmer, K. (2006). Political Decentralization and Electoral Accountability: The Argentine Experience, 1983–2001. *British Journal of Political Science* 36(1): 133–157.

Gerber, A. S. & Green, D. P. (2012). *Field Experiments*. New York: W. W. Norton & Co.

Gilbert, D. T., Giesler, R. B., & Morris, K. A. (1995). When Comparisons Arise. *Journal of Personality & Social Psychology* 69(2): 227–236.

Glennerster, R. & Takavarsha, K. (2013). *Running Randomized Evaluations*. Princeton, NJ: Princeton University Press.

Gomez, B. T. & Hansford, T. G. (2015). Economic Retrospection and the Calculus of Voting. *Political Behavior* 37(2): 309–329.

Green D. P. & Gerber, A. S. (2003). The Underprovision of Experiments in Political Science. *Annals of the American Academy of Political and Social Science* 589(1): 94–112.

Guala, F. (2005). *The Methodology of Experimental Economics*. Cambridge: Cambridge University Press.

Hansen, K. M., Olsen, A. L., & Bech, M. (2015). Cross-National Yardstick Comparisons: A Choice Experiment on a Forgotten Voter Heuristic. *Political Behavior* 37(4): 767–789.

Hart, A. & Matthews, J. S. (2022). Unmasking Accountability: Judging Performance in an Interdependent World. *Journal of Politics* 84(3): 1607–1622.

Hart, A. & Middleton, J. A. (2014). Priming under Fire: Reverse Causality and the Classic Media Priming Hypothesis. *Journal of Politics* 76(2): 581–592.

Hayes, R. C., Imai, M., & Shelton, C. A. (2015). Attribution Error in Economic Voting: Evidence from Trade Shocks. *Economic Inquiry* 53(1): 258–275.

Healy, A. & Lenz, G. S. (2014). Substituting the End for the Whole: Why Voters Respond Primarily to the Election-Year Economy. *American Journal of Political Science* 58(1): 31–47.

Healy, A. & Malhotra, N. (2013). Retrospective Voting Reconsidered. *Annual Review of Political Science* 16: 285–306.

Healy, A., Malhotra, N., & Mo, C. H. (2010). Irrelevant Events Affect Voters' Evaluations of Government Performance. *Proceedings of the National Academy of Sciences* 107(29): 12804–12809.

Hellwig, T. (2001). Interdependence, Government Constraints, and Economic Voting. *Journal of Politics* 63(4): 1141–1162.

Hellwig, T. (2008). Globalization, Policy Constraints, and Vote Choice. *Journal of Politics* 70(4): 1128–1141.

Holmstrom, B. R. (1982). Moral Hazard in Teams. *Bell Journal of Economics and Management Science* 13(2): 324–340.

Huber, G. A., Hill, S. J., & Lenz, G. S. (2012). Sources of Bias in Retrospective Decision Making: Experimental Evidence on Voters' Limitations in Controlling Incumbents. *American Political Science Review* 106(4): 720–741.

Iyengar, S. & Kinder, D. R. (1987). *News That Matters*. Chicago, IL: University of Chicago Press.

Kayser, M. A. & Peress, M. (2012). Benchmarking across Borders: Electoral Accountability and the Necessity of Comparison. *American Political Science Review* 106(3): 661–684.

Key, V. O. (1966). *The Responsible Electorate*. Cambridge, MA: Harvard University Press.

Kiewiet, D. R. & Rivers, D. (1984). A Retrospective on Retrospective Voting. *Political Behavior* 6(4): 369–393.

Klašnja, M. & Tucker, J. A. (2013). The Economy, Corruption, and the Vote: Evidence from Experiments in Sweden and Moldova. *Electoral Studies* 32 (3): 536–543.

Kuklinski, J. H. & Quirk, P. J. (2000). Reconsidering the Rational Public: Cognition, Heuristics, and Mass Opinion. In A. Lupia, M. D. McCubbins, & S. L. Popkin, eds., *Elements of Reason: Cognition, Choice, and the Bounds of Rationality.* New York: Cambridge University Press, pp. 153–182.

Larsen, M. (2019). Is the Relationship Between Political Responsibility and Electoral Accountability Causal, Adaptive and Policy-Specific? *Political Behavior* 41(4): 1071–1098.

Latour, B. (1984). *Les microbes: Guerre et paix.* Paris: Métailié [English translation: *The Pasteurization of France.* Cambridge, MA: Harvard University Press.]

Lau, R. R. (1982). Negativity in Political Perception. *Political Behavior* 4(4): 353–377.

Lau, R. R. & Redlawsk, D. P. (2001). Advantages and Disadvantages of Cognitive Heuristics in Political Decision Making. *American Journal of Political Science* 45(4): 951–971.

Lau, R. R. & Redlawsk, D. P. (2006). *How Voters Decide: Information Processing in Election Campaigns.* Cambridge: Cambridge University Press.

Leigh, A. & McLeish, M. (2009). Are State Elections Affected by the National Economy? Evidence from Australia. *Economic Record* 85(269): 210–222.

León, S. (2012). How Do Citizens Attribute Responsibility in Multilevel States? Learning, Biases and Asymmetric Federalism. Evidence from Spain. *Electoral Studies* 31(1): 120–130.

Lodge, M., McGraw, K. M., & Stroh, P. (1989). An Impression-Driven Model of Candidate Evaluation. *American Political Science Review* 83(2): 399–419.

Lodge, M. & Taber, C. S. (2013). *The Rationalizing Voter.* New York: Cambridge University Press.

Lucas, J. W. (2003). Theory-Testing, Generalization, and the Problem of External Validity. *Sociological Theory* 21(3): 236–253.

Lupia, A. & McCubbins, M. D. (1998). *The Democratic Dilemma.* Cambridge: Cambridge University Press.

Malhotra, N. & Margalit, Y. (2014). Expectation Setting and Retrospective Voting. *Journal of Politics* 76(4): 1000–1016.

McDermott, R. (2002). Experimental Methodology in Political Science. *Political Analysis* 10(4): 325–342.

Mook, D. G. (1983). In Defense of External Invalidity. *American Psychologist* 38(4): 379–387.

Moore, D. A. & Klein, W. M. P. (2008). Use of Absolute and Comparative Performance Feedback in Absolute and Comparative Judgments and Decisions. *Organizational Behavior and Human Decision Processes* 107(1): 60–74.

Mussweiler, T. (2003). Comparison Processes in Social Judgment: Mechanisms and Consequences. *Psychological Review* 110(3): 472–489.

Mutz, D. C. (2011). *Population-Based Survey Experiments*. Princeton, NJ: Princeton University Press.

Olsen, A. L. (2017). Compared to What? How Social and Historical Reference Points Affect Citizens' Performance Evaluations. *Journal of Public Administration Research and Theory* 27(4): 562–580.

Orr, L. L., Olsen, R. B., Bell, S. H. et al. (2019). Using the Results from Rigorous Multisite Evaluations to Inform Local Policy Decisions. *Journal of Policy Analysis and Management* 38: 978–1003. https://doi.org/10.1002/pam.22154.

Park, B. B. (2019). Compared to What? Media-Guided Reference Points and Relative Economic Voting. *Electoral Studies* 62: 102085.

Pereira, M. M. & Waterbury, N. W. (2019). Do Voters Discount Political Scandals over Time? *Political Research Quarterly* 72(3): 584–595.

Pérez, E. (2016). *Unspoken Politics: Implicit Attitudes and Political Thinking*. Cambridge: Cambridge University Press.

Pierce, G. L., Braga, A. A., Hyatt, R. R., & Koper, C. S. (2004). Characteristics and Dynamics of Illegal Firearms Markets: Implications for a Supply-Side Enforcement Strategy. *Justice Quarterly* 21(2): 391–422.

Plott, C. R. (1991). Will Economics Become an Experimental Science? *Southern Economic Journal* 57(4): 901–919.

Popkin. S. L. (1991). *The Reasoning Voter*. Chicago, IL: University of Chicago Press.

Powell, G. B. (2000). *Elections As Instruments of Democracy*. New Haven, CT: Yale University Press.

Pozzoni, G. & Kaidesoja, T. (2021). Context in Mechanism-Based Explanation. *Philosophy of the Social Sciences* 51(6): 523–554.

Quinn, D. P. & Woolley, J. T. (2001). Democracy and National Economic Performance: The Preference for Stability. *American Journal of Political Science* 45(3): 634–657.

Rodrik, D. (2008). The New Development Economics: We Shall Experiment, but How Shall We Learn? Harvard Kennedy School (HKS) Working Paper No. RWP08-055, http://dx.doi.org/10.2139/ssrn.1296115.

Roth, A. E. (1995). Introduction to Experimental Economics. In J. H. Kagel & A. E. Roth, eds., *The Handbook of Experimental Economics* (pp. 3–109). Princeton, NJ: Princeton University Press.

Sigelman, L., Sigelman, C. K., & Bullock, D. (1991). Reconsidering Pocketbook Voting: An Experimental Approach. *Political Behavior* 13(2): 129–149.

Simonovits, G. (2015). An Experimental Approach to Economic Voting. *Political Behavior* 37(4): 977–994.

Smith, V. L. (1962). An Experimental Study of Competitive Market Behavior. *Journal of Political Economy* 70(2): 111–137.

Sniderman, P. M., Brody, R. A., & Tetlock, P. E. (1991). *Reasoning and Choice: Explorations in Political Psychology.* New York: Cambridge University Press.

Soroka, S. (2014). *Negativity in Democratic Politics.* Cambridge: Cambridge University Press.

Soroka, S., Fournier, P., & Nir, L. (2019). Cross-National Evidence of Negativity Bias in Psychophysiological Reactions to News. *Proceedings of the National Academy of Sciences* 116: 18888–18892.

Stiers, D., Dassonneville, R., & Lewis-Beck, M. S. (2020). The Abiding Voter: The Lengthy Horizon of Retrospective Evaluations. *European Journal of Political Research* 59(3): 646–668.

Thye, S. E. (2007). Logical and Philosophical Foundations of Experimental Research in the Social Sciences. In M. Webster & J. Sell, eds., *Laboratory Experiments in the Social Sciences* (pp. 57–86). Cambridge, MA: Academic Press.

Tilley, J. & Hobolt, S. B. (2011). Is the Government to Blame? An Experimental Test of How Partisanship Shapes Perceptions of Performance and Responsibility. *Journal of Politics* 73(2): 316–330.

Zelditch, M. (2007). The External Validity of Experiments That Test Theories. In M. Webster & J. Sell, eds., *Laboratory Experiments in the Social Sciences* (pp. 87–112). Cambridge, MA: Academic Press.

Acknowledgements

The spark for this Element grew out of conversations about experimental approaches to economic voting at the University of Mannheim in summer 2017. The project has expanded and changed considerably since then, and we published what we present in this Element as Experiments 5-9 in a 2022 article in the *Journal of Politics*. We thank the editors of the *Journal of Politics* for allowing us to build on those materials here. We are grateful for the comments and support we received throughout this project. We want to thank Jamie Druckman, Eline de Rooij, and Mark Kayser for their extensive comments at a book workshop as well as C. Austin Davis, Patrick Jackson, Stuart Soroka, and several anonymous reviewers for their support and advice. Scott acknowledges the generous support of the Alexander von Humboldt Foundation and the Mannheim Centre for European Social Research at the University of Mannheim.

Cambridge Elements ⹀

Experimental Political Science

James N. Druckman
Northwestern University

James N. Druckman is the Payson S. Wild Professor of Political Science and the Associate Director of the Institute for Policy Research at Northwestern University. He served as an editor for the journals Political Psychology and Public Opinion Quarterly as well as the University of Chicago Press's series in American Politics. He currently is the co-Principal Investigator of Time-Sharing Experiments for the Social Sciences (TESS) and sits on the American National Election Studies' Board. He previously served as President of the American Political Science Association section on Experimental Research and helped oversee the launching of the Journal of Experimental Political Science. He was co-editor of the Cambridge Handbook of Experimental Political Science. He is a Fellow of the American Academy of Arts and Sciences and has published more than 100 articles/book chapters on public opinion, political communication, campaigns, research methods, and other topics.

About the Series
There currently are few outlets for extended works on experimental methodology in political science. The new Experimental Political Science Cambridge Elements series features research on experimental approaches to a given substantive topic, and experimental methods by prominent and upcoming experts in the field.

Cambridge Elements ≡

Experimental Political Science

Elements in the Series

Printed in the United States
by Baker & Taylor Publisher Services